INSIGHTS INTO
PRICING

FROM OPERATIONS RESEARCH
AND BEHAVIORAL SCIENCE

ALFRED OXENFELDT

DAVID MILLER

ABRAHAM SHUCHMAN

Graduate School of Business, Columbia University

CHARLES WINICK

J. Walter Thompson Agency

WADSWORTH PUBLISHING COMPANY

BELMONT, CALIFORNIA

L.C. Cat. Card No.: 61-15842

Printed in the United States of America

CONTENTS

INTRODUCTION

Great efforts have been made for some time to spur the introduction of behavioral science and operations research materials (hereafter sometimes termed "peripheral materials") into schools of business. As a consequence, curricula are being drastically revised, and the array of skills found in business schools is shifting perceptibly. In addition, many advertising and marketing research agencies have added specialists in behavioral science and operations research to their staffs to gain the benefits to be reaped from those fields.

The reasons behind current efforts to add behavioral science and operations research materials to business subjects are of no special practical concern, although they are not lacking in interest. However, the validity of these goals and the best methods of attaining them are of great practical importance. Even at this time, it is not clear how much the behavioral sciences and operations research can contribute to the understanding and the practice of business (although, of course, the intensive re-examination of teaching methods and course content associated with efforts to introduce these materials into business schools is highly salutary in itself). Moreover, even if these fields can enrich the functional fields of business, effective methods apparently have not yet been found to incorporate them readily into business courses.

VALIDITY OF INTRODUCING PERIPHERAL MATERIALS INTO BUSINESS SUBJECTS

Advocates of change in business courses by the introduction of contributions from behavioral science and operations research are not explicit about the benefits to be realized from following their advice. They point out that these fields are relevant to business subjects -- and who can dispute that business is concerned with human behavior and therefore falls within the province of behavioral science. They also point to spectacular successes that have been achieved by the application of mathematical techniques to certain business problems -- a very narrow range, to be sure. However, even the more ardent proponents of the "new look" in business training do not indicate whether present views will be reversed, and deep new insights and more profound understanding gained, or whether their expectations are quite modest.

What can reasonably be expected from the introduction of peripheral

materials into any field of study? To discuss this question in very general
terms is certain to be fruitless, for the answer surely varies substantially f
one subject to another. To be more specific: What can one hope to learn
about business from such fields as behavioral science and operations resea
Any answer to this question must take full account of the fact that business
both a field of study and a body of experience. An enormous fund of empiri
material is available both to businessmen and to those who study business
a result, the generalizations about business are "kept honest" by constant
comparison with experience. There can, moreover, be no question that bus
nessmen have very strong motivation to learn the lessons taught by experie
Businessmen clearly know a great deal about what happens in business, ha
thought a great deal about why it happens, have considered many alternativ
courses of action -- and have even tested many of them.

In short, business subjects have been enriched by enormous experier
and numerous opportunities to test hypotheses. Therefore, it is highly unl
that very dramatic discoveries will result from bringing to bear upon busine
subjects the tools, concepts, and approaches of other fields. Those who
pect great improvement in understanding of business or in the actions that
should be taken by businessmen are almost certain to be disappointed. Ex
tations of the gains to be realized must, therefore, be realistic. Much cou
be lost by implying that miracles will be wrought. However, some modest
but significant -- gains may be won.

One illustration will sharpen what has been said, and will suggest th
extent and form of the benefits to be achieved by introducing peripheral mat
rials into marketing. Contrary to the so-called "law of demand" and the
"popular wisdom" of marketing specialists, it sometimes happens that more
sold of a product at a high price than at a lower one. In other words, altho
business experience presents overwhelming evidence of the validity of the
of demand," it also produces some vexing exceptions. In accounting for th
exceptions, students of business have said many things: some have said t
when the products are extreme luxuries or gifts, one may sell more at a high
price than at a low one; others have said that consumers may believe that a
price has not really been reduced but, rather, that they are being offered sh
merchandise at the lower price. These explanations do not go far. They do
not explain, for example, the relationship between the effect of price chang
and the nature of luxuries and gifts, since price reductions ordinarily do increase unit sales of those products. Similarly, marked-down merchandise
usually does sell better after the markdown.

Behavioral scientists approach this phenomenon with different questic
from those asked by the economist or marketing specialist. They ask: How
will the customer perceive the changed price, and how will he perceive the
product after its price has been changed? Recognition of the difference between the reality and a customer's perception of it is central to any explana

for the upward-sloping demand curve. To formulate the problem in terms of perceptions, therefore, does help to explain why sales sometimes rise when price is increased. More important, it helps to predict when that result will take place and to suggest what businessmen might do to correct or to foster misperceptions. In other words, behavioral science leads us to ask whether the customer actually perceives a price reduction when price is cut on some products or recognizes price increases when they have taken place. Behavioral science findings suggest that customers may actually misperceive reality and "see" a change in the quality of merchandise that offsets the effect of a price change. Thus, of two similar products, the one sold at a higher price is sometimes perceived as being worth more per dollar than the one offered at the lower price.

Much more could be said about this example, but enough has been said, perhaps, to illustrate the kind of contribution that one can expect from peripheral fields such as behavioral science and operations research. These fields are unlikely to uncover wholly new phenomena, or to explain fully or along wholly original lines why any puzzling business phenomenon occurs. On the other hand, they may sometimes provide, as in the foregoing illustration, a concept or a "model" that is more powerful than the explanatory concepts previously employed and, as a consequence, may even suggest effective courses of action that were not apparent before. Of course, to test the value of any contributions drawn from related fields, one must expose them to the businessman or the consultant and see if he can "do anything extra" with them. In this case, behavioral science seems to enable the businessman to predict more successfully than before when the demand curve for a product will slope upward.

Such accretions to an understanding of business are very worthwhile; if they are numerous, total understanding of business doctrine will expand considerably. Thus, even though no startling discoveries can be anticipated from the introduction of behavioral science and operations research into business subjects, many cases of deeper understanding and occasional improvements in ability to forecast can be expected.

The foregoing pages help to explain why the research project that formed the basis for this book was based on the conviction that business subjects can gain, although only moderately, from the introduction of materials from the behavioral sciences and operations research. The main purpose of the book, however, is not to indicate the nature and magnitude of those gains. Rather -- because of the authors' conviction that the methods being employed to introduce peripheral materials into business are slow and inefficient -- it represents the results of a team effort to test a new method of uncovering relevant materials in peripheral fields and of acquainting teachers, advanced students, and executives with developments that have particular relevance to one test field.

METHODS OF INCORPORATING PERIPHERAL
MATERIALS INTO THE STUDY OF BUSINESS

In current efforts to introduce operations research and behavioral science materials into business schools and into agencies serving business, two methods have been most widely employed: (1) Specialists in these peripheral fields have been added to staffs in the expectation that their expertise will "rub off" on other staff members. (2) Specialists have been invited to give courses in their specialty in the expectation that those who take these courses will make applications to business. These measures have achieved very limited success, as far as one can determine -- although it is extremely difficult to appraise them. Both of these methods would "tack on" related disciplines as if they were ornaments that add luster to a business school curriculum or to a consulting agency. Their weakness consists in their failure to incorporate into business materials the wisdom of peripheral fields wherever and whenever these fields contribute to better understanding. Generally, it appears, these methods serve to create nagging reservations about the validity of some generalizations contained in business writings, or to suggest interesting areas for special study for those few who have the inclination to conduct business research. Although these consequences are not to be depreciated, much more must be achieved to justify the efforts and outlays already made and yet to be made.

This book is the outgrowth of a different approach to the transplanting of peripheral materials to the field of business. The approach, called the "team method" for want of a better term, emphasizes two objectives: (1) the need to select carefully, from the mass of possibilities, the materials most relevant to the study of business; and (2) the need to communicate the materials selected in a form that incorporates them within and makes direct application to the relevant fields of business.

This book was produced by a team of four: an operations research specialist and two marketing specialists -- David Miller, Abraham Shuchman, and myself (respectively), Graduate School of Business, Columbia University; and a behavioral scientist -- Charles Winick, J. Walter Thompson Agency, New York. The specialists in the fields of operations research and behavioral science combed the literature in their areas of specialization to discover materials that might improve understanding of pricing, either now or in the not-too-distant future. They discussed their findings with and made recommendations to the marketing specialists. As an outgrowth of these discussions, manuscripts were prepared, which, after numerous revisions and emendations, turned into the pages that follow.

It is not suggested that the field of pricing is representative of all business subjects or that the work of the team that produced this book is representative of what other teams would have brought forth. Our work does, nevertheless, represent a partial test of another method of incorporating peripheral materials into the business schools and the agencies serving business.

It is difficult to indicate precisely which member of the team is responsible for each part of the book, for many parts were truly hammered out by two or more members of the group. As a rough summary, the chapters dealing with operations research (Part One) were prepared by David Miller with relatively little assistance from the rest of the team; the sections of Part Two that review behavioral science doctrine were prepared primarily by Charles Winick; and I wrote most of the sections that discuss possible applications of behavioral science to pricing. Abraham Shuchman read all sections of the manuscript, participated in most of the discussions, and made numerous valuable suggestions at many points.

The team wishes to acknowledge its debt to Professor Paul Lazarsfeld, who was most generous with his time and whose counsel was extremely helpful.

Cooperation among several persons inevitably involves compromise. Many things included here are not stated exactly as each individual member of the team would have written them. As director of the team -- and not an entirely permissive and democratic one at that -- I assume responsibility for any errors, both of broad concept and of detail, that may appear.

Alfred R. Oxenfeldt

PART ONE

OPERATIONS RESEARCH FINDINGS

RELEVANT TO PRICING

In considering new developments that might be relevant to pricing problems, we can hardly overlook one latecomer to the field of business analysis. One of the most striking business phenomena of recent years has been the rapid growth of something called "operations research." Indications of this growth are everywhere: seminars on operations research for executives; books on operations research; want ads for operations research analysts; management consultants specializing in operations research; business-magazine articles devoted to operations research; courses on operations research offered in business schools and in industrial engineering departments; and even, in one or two cases, whole college departments devoted to operations research. This phenomenal growth results from the belief that somehow operations research provides solutions for many complicated business problems that were previously unsolvable. What, if anything, is different and "better" about operations research than the methods ordinarily used to solve business problems?

It is easy to get "answers" to this question; but, unfortunately, many are flatly contradictory. At one extreme are a large number of experienced business theoreticians and practitioners who say: "What's operations research? It's just a new name, a gimmick to get some consultant fees out of companies. We've been doing the same thing for years -- without the fancy title." At the other extreme, many operations research practitioners answer: "Nonsense! Most operations research methods are new developments -- ten or fifteen years old at most. And the majority of problems we handle couldn't be handled without these new methods. Every new development has roots in the past, and operations research is no exception. But there is a fundamentally new approach to business problems involved in it."

Which of these two points of view is correct? Before this can be answered, it is necessary to learn what operations research is. Unfortunately, there is no consensus among its practitioners; no definition is generally accepted. Perhaps the most common one would go like this: "Operations research is the application of scientific method to business problems and the use of quantitative methods in business decisions." This definition sounds reasonable, but it isn't very illuminating. Cost accounting and quality control are two well-known techniques that meet this definition, so it is clear that the definition does not uniquely describe operations research.

But perhaps this is the wrong approach. Definitions are always difficult and not always illuminating. And, after all, as Polonius puts it in Hamlet, "For to define true madness, What is it but to be nothing else but mad?" Analogously, some of its practitioners have said that operations research is simply what operations research practitioners do. Granting this, a reasonable first step would be to briefly discuss what these practitioners have done. In short, what is the history of operations research?

Operations research got its start, and its name, during World War II. Military commanders, faced with the necessity of making numerous crucial operational decisions, discovered (quite by accident) that scientists from various disciplines could often help in solving complicated military problems. This discovery was made when the British military command could not explain the unexpectedly large losses of bomber planes in its earliest mass-bombing raids on Germany. Some physicists who heard of the problem suggested an ingenious solution to it. As a result of this success, further problems were presented to these physicists, and soon groups of scientists were formed especially to deal with such problems. By the time the United States entered the war, there were many such groups, and they were known by the name of "OR teams." The United States -- reasoning that if physicists could solve command problems, other scientists should also make major contributions -- established many OR groups for each of the branches of the military. A variety of scientists were soon involved in the OR groups: chemists, psychologists, sociologists, mathematicians, economists, logicians, even philosophers.

What kinds of problems were these OR groups given to solve? Put in the form of questions, some of them were: What are the best methods for searching for enemy submarines? What should be the setting on depth bombs dropped by planes? What size of convoys should be sent across the Atlantic? Should merchant vessels have anti-aircraft guns on them? What are the best defensive tactics against kamikaze (suicide plane) attacks? What should be the defensive tactics of destroyers protecting a convoy against enemy submarines? What is the best allocation of planes against enemy submarines?

Because of their undoubted success with these military problems, the question arose as to just what these groups were doing that was different. The novel features of the OR military experience received most emphasis. One such was the team approach -- the use of a group of scientists of diverse backgrounds pooling their efforts on some problem not directly related to any one of their specialties.

Many early discussions of OR practically equated it with the team approach. Another feature emphasized was the type of problem attacked. Generally, the problems were ones that arose from the need of some military leader to make decisions. Often these problems had been traditionally handled by judgment or informed intuition -- and the OR solutions to them were sometimes diametrically opposed to the judgmental solutions.

A third feature of OR was its method of attacking the problem. This method was almost always quantitative, and usually involved the construction and solution of mathematical equations -- a mathematical "model" of the problem -- set up in an attempt to describe the problem.

Some of the military OR experts believed that the methods which had had successful military applications should be equally applicable to the problems of business and industry. After the war ended, they attempted to demonstrate the effectiveness of OR when applied to business problems. They induced some large companies to hire OR experts on a permanent basis. Soon the large management-consultant organizations added OR to the bag of tricks they offered, at a price, to business. An OR society was formed, several journals devoted to the subject were founded, and increasing attention was paid to this new field in various business publications. A steady subsequent increase in OR practitioners and in OR activities has, in recent years, led to the final capstone of success: some business schools have added courses on OR to their curricula and sometimes even degrees in OR.

The use of OR by business has clarified and changed some of the ideas about the nature of OR which resulted from its military applications. One of the three features mentioned above has proved to be dispensable: the team approach. Businesses are employing individuals to apply OR methods to certain kinds of problems. On a novel or complex problem, it may be preferable to engage more than one person. However, the benefits of team efforts and the pooling of diverse backgrounds are not unique to OR. Rather, they are true of most human efforts and, in particular, no more true of OR than of, say, chemistry. Unfortunately, the idea that OR is somehow synonymous with the team approach continues to be promulgated.[1] The businessman should be reassured that one man can perfectly well utilize OR methods. There is no need for a mystical OR analogue to the ancient Gnostic belief in the peculiar efficacy of a community of believers.

----

[1]There may be some vested interest involved here. Large consultant organizations which have such teams available may well be gratified by emphasis on the team approach. But the businessman who is considering the possible applicability of OR to his organization may well find the thought of a team of high-priced experts an overly chastening one.

The other two above-mentioned features of OR have stood up better under the test of business experience. First, OR methods continue to be utilized on problems that require resolution by executive decision. Second, the mainstay of all OR methods remains the utilization of mathematics and the construction of mathematical models. As a matter of fact, mathematical methods and models play such an important role in OR that many presentations of the subject are organized around the various mathematical techniques that are frequently utilized.

Now let us return to our original question: Is operations research something new or isn't it? As is often the case, the truth is probably somewhere between the two opposing positions. The side that says OR is "just a new name" is partially right. The great majority of the concepts used by operations research specialists in setting up and solving business problems are the well-known, tried-and-true economic mainstays: opportunity costs, sunk costs, out-of-pocket costs, elasticities, etc. Business analysts have been using these same notions since they were first introduced, and operations research is no exception. On the other hand, operations research has unquestionably succeeded in utilizing these concepts in the solution of all sorts of problems that were absolutely unsolvable twenty years ago. Further, it has developed new techniques of mathematical analysis, which permit entirely new kinds of problems to be formulated and solved. Finally, some of the ideas worked out in operations research are sufficiently novel to justify calling them new conceptualizations. Certainly these differences are "new."

We can leave the resolution of this semantic question to the tastes of the individual. In the next three sections, we will present some operations research ideas that have particular relevance for pricing problems. The reader can decide for himself whether or not the ideas are new. In any event, we think he will find them insightful and useful in the consideration of pricing problems.

CHAPTER I

DECISION THEORY

Executives are concerned essentially with making the "right" or the
st" decision. They must decide how much to charge for products, whether
where to open a new plant, how much money to allocate for advertising,
. In each case the executive hopes to make the "best" decision. In recent
rs a considerable body of theory has been developed about decision making;
us see what decision theory can tell us about decision problems in pricing.

We should recognize at the outset that decision theory does not apply
ricing problems any more than it applies to other problems requiring
cutive decision. Therefore, we cannot hope to learn anything specific
i it about pricing problems. But in this respect decision theory is not
erent from much of economic theory. Economic theory may not indicate
ctly what price to charge for a product; but it does help to understand the
lications of any particular price, and it provides a framework to help in
king about pricing problems. Although it doesn't "solve" pricing problems,
oes provide considerable assistance. We can hope that decision theory
. provide us with insights that will be similarly helpful in a different area.

MULATION OF A DECISION PROBLEM

We shall first consider some extremely simple decision problems as a
is for reviewing some of the essential propositions of decision theory.
pose Mr. X, who has $1,000 that he is willing to invest, is offered an
ortunity to invest this amount in either of two government securities: A or
Suppose the yield on security A is 4% per year, and the yield on security B
$\frac{1}{2}$% per year. Assume, further, that these securities are "cast iron" and
there is no risk of loss or nonpayment of interest. To complete our
cription of Mr. X's situation, let us add that he cannot invest in anything
e. If he chooses not to invest in one of these securities, his only alterna-
is to leave his money in the bank, where it draws interest of 3% per year.

Mr. X has a decision problem, although an extremely simple one. He
three choices, or possible decisions: (1) Do not invest. (2) Invest in

security A. (3) Invest in security B.

It may seem obvious that Mr. X should make his third possible decision: invest in security B. Those to whom this decision seems obvious would probably reason as follows: If Mr. X leaves his money in the bank, he will get a return of $30 per year; if he invests in security A he will get a return of $40 per year; and if he invests in security B, he will get a return of $45 per year. Since his largest possible return is $45 per year, from an investment in security B, it follows that this is the decision he should make. We immediately see two steps in this reasoning: (1) Determine the outcomes of the various possible courses of action. (2) Choose the course of action that offers the greatest return. We will shortly discover that a third, and very important, step was also involved; but first let us note that these two steps are generally found in every decision problem. In decision theory we call these steps, respectively, the determination of the payoff for each possible course of action, and the establishment of a decision criterion. For convenience, we call each possible course of action a strategy. With this terminology established, we can formulate Mr. X's decision problem very compactly:

		Payoff
Strategy 1:	Do not invest.	$30 per year
Strategy 2:	Invest in security A.	$40 per year
Strategy 3:	Invest in security B.	$45 per year

Suggested decision criterion: Choose the strategy with the largest payoff.

Our example illustrates these two ideas: payoff and decision criteria. We will see shortly that the seemingly simple notion of payoff conceals a number of complexities and that there are many different decision criteria; the reader, therefore, should not be misled by the simplicity of this first example. But before we proceed with a discussion of these difficulties, we must see whether we have really described all the relevant features of Mr. X's decision problem.

Can we be certain that Mr. X wants simply to get the greatest possible return? Obviously, persons faced with decision problems similar to that of Mr. X often do make the decision that will give them the greatest possible return. But this is not necessarily the case. For a number of reasons, Mr. X may not be willing to choose the third strategy even though it gives the greatest return. For example, he may ascribe considerable importance to having his money immediately available, and it may be difficult to convert holdings of security B into cash. In this event, Mr. X could with complete rationality reject the conclusion that he should choose the third strategy. How can we recast our formulation of the decision problem so that we can include such possibilities?

CONSIDERATION OF OBJECTIVES IN DETERMINING PAYOFF

If we asked Mr. X to criticize our presentation of his decision problem, he would probably say that our mistake lay in having assumed that he is interested only in return on investment. He would take exception to the hidden assumption that the _payoff_ is identical with return on investment. He would tell us that sometimes this is his only consideration but that often other factors also enter the picture. It is clear, then, that we must incorporate such alternative possibilities into our description of the decision problem. Mr. X has told us that we have to take account of what he wants to _accomplish_ by making a decision -- or, in the usual terminology of decision theory, we have to consider his _objective_ or _objectives_. Now, how do different objectives affect our description of the decision problem?

Mr. X's criticism is really quite obvious, at least after it has been pointed out. In homely language, it amounts to saying that if Mr. X is interested in getting apples as a result of his decision, then we cannot accomplish anything by counting how many oranges he will get. Knowledge of Mr. X's objective tells us whether to count apples or oranges. In our picture of the decision problem, therefore, a change in objectives will be expressed by different payoffs. The payoff will have to be measured in terms of apples, oranges, or grapefruit, depending on Mr. X's objective. To put it more formally, the objective determines the scale of values against which the payoff is measured. The structure of our example, in these terms, is:

Objective: To get maximum return.

Payoff: Return per year.

Decision criterion: Choose strategy with largest payoff.

This was the way we handled the problem before we had the benefit of Mr. X's criticism. If he now tells us that he has a different objective, our problem will look like this:

Objective: ?

Payoff: ?

Decision criterion: Choose strategy with largest payoff.

The point is that if the payoff is defined, as it must be, in terms of the objective, then the decision criterion need not be changed. Of course, the decision criterion could equally be: "Choose strategy with smallest payoff." Usually, we would simply select the most convenient way of measuring the payoff for a given objective. For example, we might measure the payoff in terms of loss, in which case we would want to minimize the payoff; or in terms of gain, in which case we would want to maximize it.

Let us suppose that Mr. X is more specific. He tells us that he believes an investment should return him at least 5% per year. Otherwise, he prefers a return of 3% combined with the advantage of having his money immediately available to him. Thus -- since he prefers to accept a 3% return plus ready availability to anything less than a 5% return without ready availability -- Mr. X ascribes a value of 2% to having his money readily available. We can now formulate his decision problem along the lines indicated above:

Objective: To get the greatest value.

Payoff: Return per year, counting ready availability as worth
                  2% per year.

                                                    Payoff
Strategy 1:   Do not invest in securities.   5%

Strategy 2:   Invest in security A.   4%

Strategy 3:   Invest in security B. $4\frac{1}{2}$%

Decision criterion: Choose strategy with largest payoff.

The use of this decision criterion, of course, results in the choice of strategy 1. Under Mr. X's stated objective, strategies 2 and 3 would actually lose him value, compared to holding his funds in a savings account.

Our discussion has emphasized the central position that the payoff occupies in the decision problem. It is therefore important that we consider some of the difficulties involved in suitably defining the payoff in terms of the objective.

QUANTITATIVE AND NONQUANTITATIVE EXPRESSIONS OF PAYOFF

As we proceed further in our consideration of decision problems, it will become evident that most of the conclusions we can reach depend upon some sort of arithmetical manipulation of the payoffs of the various strategies. In order to manipulate something arithmetically, we must be able to express it quantitatively. Is there any reason to believe that the payoff can always be expressed in quantitative terms? Unfortunately, no: for some objectives, it is simply impractical to express the payoff quantitatively; but for other objectives, it may well be impossible, even in theory, to determine a quantitative payoff. Suppose, for example, that executives are faced with a decision in regard to diversification and that their objectives are to get a satisfactory return on investment, maximum long-range security, and a minimum of worry. How can one possibly determine a valid quantitative payoff for such a decision problem? The payoffs in many decision problems involve precisely such difficulties. In fact, it is sometimes maintained that almost all "important" decisions involve nonquantifiable factors. If this is true, we cannot hope to gain much assistance from decision theory. Fortunately, however, it seems probable that a considerable number of the decision problems of business can be expressed quantitatively.

One possibility is available even if the payoff is nonquantifiable: to achieve a <u>ranking</u> of the payoffs instead of a quantitative measure of them. Thus, for a different objective, Mr. X might be able to say that he preferred payoff 2 to payoff 3, even though he could not give quantitative values for either payoff. Such a ranking of payoffs is much less useful than quantitative expressions, but some general conclusions based on rankings can be achieved in decision theory. The limitations of ranking of payoffs are obvious, since the majority of arithmetical manipulations have no meaning when applied to rankings. For example, if three payoffs are ranked, in order of preference, 1, 2, 3, we cannot tell whether the difference in preferences for 1 and 2 is greater or less than the difference in preferences for 2 and 3. Would the ranker prefer 2 and 3 together, as compared to 1 alone? We cannot tell from the rankings. Apart from these difficulties, there are considerable problems involved in determining the rankings empirically.

We cannot deal very extensively here with the problems of rankings. Fortunately, there is a large body of literature devoted to the subject, and we refer the interested reader to this literature for further discussion. For our purposes, it is sufficient to point out that this possibility does exist for nonquantitative payoffs.

The existence of such difficulties as these makes it particularly pleasant when we have a decision problem in which the payoff can be expressed quantitatively -- for example, in terms of dollars profit, or net return on investment, or percentage share of the market. But the advantages and conveniences of these cases must not tempt us to force a given decision problem into an inappropriate mold. If certain factors involved in the objective lead to a nonquantifiable payoff, we must reconcile ourselves to the resulting difficulties -- including the possibility that the problem may be unsolvable within the framework of decision theory.

DETERMINATION OF UTILITY OF MONEY

Even where the payoff seems to be clearly quantitative, our problems are not over. It may well be that the obvious quantitative units cannot be used directly as the measure for the payoffs. For example, consider a speculative investment of $1,000. Suppose two men are faced with the decision problem of whether or not to make this investment. Suppose, further, that one of these men has only $2,000 and the other has $50,000. Will both of these men necessarily make the same decision? It seems evident that both of these men might behave rationally and yet choose different strategies. But if this is true, it follows that a straightforward expression of payoff in terms of the return from the investment would not completely describe the decision problem. It will be worthwhile to investigate this problem a little further.

To make the problem sufficiently specific, we will suppose that there is a known probability of 0.6 (6 chances out of 10) that the investment will be successful and will return a profit of $1,000. Correspondingly, there is a probability of 0.4 (4 chances out of 10) that the investment will be a total loss, thus costing the $1,000 invested. In a later section,[1] we show that situations like this one, involving probabilities of gains or losses, demand the use of expected values. We will not duplicate that discussion here but will simply point out that, in the present example, we will be guided by the <u>expected value</u> of this investment. Since the investor will gain $1,000 with a probability of 0.6 (60% of the time, if the investment were repeated many times) and will lose $1,000 with a probability of 0.4 (40% of the time), it follows that the expected value of the investment is 0.6 ($1,000) - 0.4 ($1,000) = $200. Thus, if an investor were to make this identical investment repeatedly, he could expect to receive, over a large number of such investments, an average profit of $200 per investment. For this example we will confine our prospective investor to two possible decisions: invest, or do not invest. We will further assume that he gets no return at all if he does not invest. We can now formulate a decision problem:

Objective: To get a maximum return.

Payoff: Expected return.

		Payoff
Strategy 1:	Do not invest.	0
Strategy 2:	Invest.	$200

Decision criterion: Choose strategy with largest payoff.

Clearly, with this criterion and formulation, the investor should make the investment; and he can expect, in the sense of expected values, a return of $200 from his investment. All that our reasoning tells us is that this investment is a "good bet" and that, under the stated circumstances, anyone should be willing to make the investment.

---

[1]See pages 45-48.

This formulation of the decision problem, then, leads to the conclusion that anyone should make the investment, as long as he has $1,000. Yet, when we initiated this example, we indicated that all investors probably would not choose the same strategy. In particular, it seems reasonable that an investor with more money would be willing to take some risks that an investor with less money would forego -- and both investors would be behaving "rationally." How can we set up this decision problem so that this possibility will be indicated? As the reader might expect on the basis of our discussion so far, it is a question of determining a suitable payoff.

The problem we are dealing with is one of most respectable antiquity. It is the problem of the utility of money. In our previous formulation of the decision problem, we assumed that the utility of money was the same for everyone, regardless of how much money he had to start with. This is, of course, a most questionable assumption. It is far more likely that $1,000 has more utility to an individual with only $2,000 than to an individual with $50,000. More than two hundred years ago, Bernoulli suggested that the utility of money should be considered proportional to the amount the individual already has. This is the simplest assumption one can make to reflect the smaller utility of a given amount of money to an individual who has more money originally. On this basis, for example, a gain of 10% of initial capital will have the same utility for everyone -- whether the initial capital was $2,000 or $50,000. Another result of this assumption is that the loss of utility resulting from a loss of $1,000 is always greater than the gain of utility from a gain of $1,000. These seem to be reasonable statements about the utility of money, at least to a first approximation. Our problem, then, is to find some measure of the utility of money which has these characteristics. The simplest and most convenient mathematical device that has these characteristics is logarithms.[2] We propose, therefore, to use the logarithm of a given sum of money as the measure of the utility associated with that amount of money. The reader does not need to know anything about logarithms in order to follow our reasoning. Suffice it to say that we are assuming the utility of money is measured by the logarithm of the amount. For any amount, we can look up the

---

[2]The reader who is familiar with logarithms will remember that the logarithm of the product of two numbers equals the sum of the logarithms of the two numbers. For example, the logarithm of 2 is 0.30103, and the logarithm of 2 x 2 = 4 is 0.30103 + 0.30103 = 0.60206. Now, suppose that one man has $1,000 and another man has $10,000, and that each succeeds in doubling his capital. What happens to their respective utilities? The man with $1,000 has utility equal to the logarithm of $1,000, or 3. Doubling his capital gives him a utility equal to the logarithm of $2,000, which is 3 + 0.30103 = 3.30103. The man with $10,000 has utility equal to the logarithm of $10,000, or 4. When he doubles his capital, he has utility equal to the logarithm of $20,000, or 4 + 0.30103 = 4.30103. Each man has gained the same amount of utility (an additional 0.30103) even though the additional amounts of money gained are different ($1,000 and $10,000). This example demonstrates that utility, measured by logarithms, does have one of the properties mentioned above.

logarithm in a table.

We are going to use this idea in defining a payoff for our decision problem. The reader should be perfectly clear concerning our reasoning. We maintain that the utility of money depends on the amount the individual has: $1,000 has more utility to an individual with $2,000 than it has to an individual with $50,000. We do not know the empirical relationship of the utility of money to the amount already possessed. Nonetheless, we want to illustrate the effect that such a relationship would have on the decision problem we are considering. Therefore, we are following Bernoulli in choosing the simplest relationship that will reflect the fact that the utility of a given amount of money decreases in direct proportion to increases in the amount of money already possessed. (We achieve this result, conveniently, by measuring the utility of a given amount of money by its logarithm.) We are not assuming that this use of the logarithm as a measure of utility represents in any way an approximation to the empirical relationship. It will simply be used to illustrate the effect that such considerations have on the decision problem.

The calculations are extremely easy. We will now have separate presentations of the decision problem for the man with $2,000 and for the man with $50,000. Consider the man with $2,000. We base our calculations on the utilities of the sums of money he will have if he makes the investment and wins, and if he makes the investment and loses. If he makes the investment and wins, he will have $3,000; and the utility will be measured by the logarithm of $3,000, which is 3.47712. If he loses, he will have $1,000; and the utility will be measured by the logarithm of $1,000, which is 3.00000. Since the probability of winning is 0.6 and the probability of losing is 0.4, the expected utility from the investment is

$$0.6 (3.47712) + 0.4 (3.00000) = 3.28627.$$

The number whose logarithm is 3.28627 is $1,933. This means that if he repeated this investment a large number of times, he could expect, on the average, to have the utility of a sum of money equal to $1,933 result from each such investment. We can now present the decision problem in the usual format:

Objective: To get the maximum utility, where utility is measured by the logarithm of the sum of money.

Payoff: Expected utility, measured by logarithm of sum of money.

		Payoff
Strategy 1:	Do not invest.	3.30103 (log. of $2,000)
Strategy 2:	Invest.	3.28627

Decision criterion: Choose strategy with largest payoff.

Clearly, the conclusion is that strategy 1 should be chosen: the investment should not be made. We do not have to present the payoffs in the form of logarithms. We can equally well convert the logarithms into dollars and present the decision problem thus:

Objective: To get the maximum utility, where utility is measured by the logarithm of the sum of money.

Payoff: Expected utility, measured in dollars.

	Payoff
Strategy 1: Do not invest.	$2,000
Strategy 2: Invest.	$1,933

Decision criterion: Choose strategy with largest payoff.

The conclusion is, of course, the same, since it is a matter of indifference whether we choose to express the payoff directly in logarithms or to look up in a table the numbers that have those logarithms. In either case the payoff is calculated the same way, in accordance with the objective.

Now let us consider the man with $50,000. If he makes the investment and wins, the resulting utility will be that of $51,000, measured by the logarithm of $51,000, or 4.70757. If he loses, he will have $49,000 with utility equal to the logarithm of $49,000, or 4.69020. His expected utility will therefore be

$$0.6 (4.70757) + 0.4 (4.69020) = 4.70062.$$

The number whose logarithm is 4.70062 is $50,190. We therefore present his decision problem thus:

Objective: To get the maximum utility, where utility is measured by the logarithm of the sum of money.

Payoff: Expected utility, measured in dollars.

	Payoff
Strategy 1: Do not invest.	$50,000
Strategy 2: Invest.	$50,190

Decision criterion: Choose strategy with largest payoff.

The conclusion here is that strategy 2 should be chosen: the investment should be made.

We see, then, that the introduction of the idea of the relationship of the utility of money to the amount possessed has resulted in different strategies for the two men: that is, by changing the statement of the objective, with a resulting change in the method of calculation of the payoff, we obtained these different results. The reader may or may not agree that this formulation is more reasonable than our original formulation. We simply wanted to illustrate that this possibility does exist, and that it is necessary to consider, in any particular decision problem, whether the payoff should be expressed in the obvious quantitative units of the problem.

We have discussed the complexities of the payoff at some length because it is very important to realize that the payoff need not be expressed in any particular units or, indeed, in quantifiable units at all. If the analysis of a particular decision problem is to be valid, the payoff must be in accord with the objectives of the person making the decision. If this can be accomplished, then decision theory may afford some valuable insights concerning the particular decision problem being analyzed. In our further discussion we will not refer to these difficulties. Rather, we will present various decision problems in any payoff units that happen to be convenient, since we will be interested in presenting some of the basic results of decision theory; and these results are independent of the payoffs used. The reader should not forget, however, the host of difficulties involved in establishing the payoffs for a particular problem.

DECISION CRITERIA FOR COMPLEX PROBLEMS

Let us now return to Mr. X and his investment problems. Our examples of his decision problem have been ridiculously simple. Why? First of all, in any practical case Mr. X would have had far more possible strategies available to him than the three we gave. However, it should be clear that the addition of possible strategies introduces nothing new into the problem. A little more calculation would be required, but our ultimate payoff table would have the same form as the ones we gave. There would be a greater number of rows, but we could use the same decision criterion and simply choose the strategy that had the greatest payoff, as before. Therefore, an increase in the number of possible strategies provides no new conceptual problems. The second objection to the simplicity of our examples is more serious: that is, there is not just one payoff for each strategy; on the contrary, there are usually a great number of possible payoffs, and the occurrence of any one of these payoffs is determined by factors outside the control of the person making the decision. For example, there might be two possible payoffs for each of Mr. X's possible strategies, depending on whether there is war or peace. Generally, of course, there may be a large number of such possibilities. It turns out that the necessary extensions of our decision problem, which are entailed by this objection, lead to all sorts of new considerations.

Before we develop a method for presenting this kind of decision problem, let us emphasize that these are the realistic problems. A farmer has three crops that he can plant (his three strategies); there will be a number of possible payoffs for each strategy, depending on the actual weather conditions, during the growing season. An oil company might select from among a variety of strategies for allocating its resources in foreign countries; the payoffs for each strategy depend partly on future political conditions in the countries in question. A company has a variety of strategies for locating new plants; the payoffs for the various strategies depend on national economic conditions and on specific local conditions in the future, such as availability and cost of labor. In short, the <u>typical</u> decision problem involves a number of possible payoffs for each strategy, depending on conditions that are <u>outside the control of the person making the decision</u>. We must now consider how we can represent and analyze this sort of decision problem.

We wish to incorporate a number of possible payoffs for each strategy into our representation of the decision problem. Since we are already using the rows of our payoff table to represent the possible strategies, it is natural to introduce columns that will represent the possible payoffs for each strategy. These payoffs depend on factors outside the control of the person making the decision -- the things that happen in the outside world or, as they are customarily called, "states of nature." In our payoff table, we propose, then, to represent strategies by rows, and states of nature by columns. We will denote the various strategies by S1, S2, S3, etc.; the various states of nature by N1, N2, N3, etc.; and the payoffs that will result if a particular strategy is chosen <u>and</u> a particular state of nature occurs by $P(S1, N1)$, $P(S1, N2)$, $P(S2, N2)$, etc. Then our payoff table will look like this:

	N1	N2	N3	N4	...
S1	$P(S1, N1)$	$P(S1, N2)$	$P(S1, N3)$	$P(S1, N4)$	...
S2	$P(S2, N1)$	$P(S2, N2)$	$P(S2, N3)$	$P(S2, N4)$	...
S3	$P(S3, N1)$	$P(S3, N2)$	$P(S3, N3)$	$P(S3, N4)$	...

Thus, if strategy 3 (S3) is chosen and the fourth state of nature (N4) occurs, the payoff will be $P(S3, N4)$. The number of rows and columns in the table will depend, of course, on the particular problem being analyzed; and without changing the format of the payoff table, we can include as many as are required. In our previous examples of Mr. X's decision problem, we had only one column, since we allowed for only one possible state of nature. In the payoff table on page 12, we see that we have, in these terms, $P(S1, N1)$ = $30 per year; $P(S2, N1)$ = $40 per year; and $P(S3, N1)$ = $45 per year.

Let us immediately illustrate the new difficulties that are created by this extention of the decision problem. Suppose we go back to Mr. X's original problem and assume, now, that the information we used is valid only if there is peace. Suppose that if there were war Mr. X would still receive 3% interest by leaving his money in the bank, but his return from security A (S2) would be only 2% and his return from security B (S3) would be zero. If we let N1 represent peace and N2 represent war, we have the following presentation of the decision problem:

Objective: To get maximum return.

Payoff: Return per year.

	N1	N2
S1	$30	$30
S2	$40	$20
S3	$45	0

Decision criterion: ?

We see that the representation of the decision problem is straightforward enough. The objective remains the same and the payoff remains the same (calculated the same way). But what should Mr. X use for a decision criterion?

Perhaps the reader's first thought will be that there is not enough information to choose a strategy. Specifically, he may want to know the probabilities of there being peace and war. Let us answer by saying that usually Mr. X will not know the probabilities of the various states of nature, but that we will here explore the decision criterion under the assumption that the two states of nature are equally probable -- i.e., the probability of either state's occuring is 1/2. (We may add as a parenthetical remark that almost 200 years ago Thomas Bayes proposed that if one does not know the probabilities of the different states of nature, he should assume them to be equally likely. This proposal is known as Bayes' hypothesis, and the debate on its merits has been going on vigorously ever since -- with no sign of a resolution yet in sight.)

Now that we have agreed to assume that the two states of nature are equally likely, what decision criterion should Mr. X use? The interesting answer is that there is no "best" criterion. The particular criterion chosen depends largely on one's basic attitude toward life. There are a number of equally defensible criteria, which often lead to different choices of strategy, and one is free to choose among these criteria on the basis of personal predilection. We will proceed to discuss some of the possibilities for decision criteria.

Instead of using Mr. X's decision problem above for our example, we will use a new one. If the reader desires, he can try out the various criteria on Mr. X's problem. Our example was chosen because it illustrates particularly well the different results that occur when different decision criteria are used. The reader should now be aware that the heart of the decision problem lies in the payoff table. Therefore, we will simply give the payoff table without presenting a verbal description of the problem. It could equally well represent the decision problem of an investor, a farmer, an oil company, or anyone else.[3] The decision problem is:

Objective: To get the maximum profit.

Payoff: Expected profit.

	N1	N2	N3	N4
S1	2	2	0	1
S2	1	1	1	1
S3	0	4	0	0
S4	1	3	0	0

Decision criterion: To be discussed.

Thus, if the decision is to use strategy 1 (S1) and state of nature 4 (N4) occurs, then the payoff P(S1, N4) will be 1. There are four possible strategies and four possible states of nature. The payoffs are in dollars and they could equally well be considered to be in much larger units. The problem is to choose a strategy. What possible decision criteria might be used?

One reasonable procedure might be to determine the average payoff for each strategy and choose the strategy that has the largest average payoff. The average payoff is, of course, simply the expected value of the payoff over all possible states of nature; it is calculated just as any other expected value is calculated. For example, the average payoff for S1 is simply $(2 + 2 + 0 + 1)/4 = 1.25$. Similarly, the average payoff for S2 is $(1 + 1 + 1 + 1)/4 = 1$. In this way we get the following table:

_____

[3]The particular payoff table we will use comes from an example in John Milnor's "Games Against Nature," in Decision Processes, ed. R. M. Thrall, C. H. Coombs, and K. R. Davis (New York: John Wiley & Sons, 1954), p. 50.

	Average payoff
S1	1.25
S2	1
S3	1
S4	1

The decision criterion of choosing the strategy that has the largest average payoff is called the Laplace criterion. By Laplace's criterion we should choose S1.

Another criterion is that of Abraham Wald. Let us ask: What is the worst we can do with each strategy? Clearly, the worst we can do with any particular strategy is the minimum payoff in the row for that strategy. Thus, if we choose S1, the worst that can happen is that N3 should occur, in which case we would get a payoff of zero. If we choose S2, the worst that can happen is that we will get a return of 1, since this is the return for each state of nature. We easily get the following table:

	Minimum payoff
S1	0
S2	1
S3	0
S4	0

Wald's criterion is that we should select the strategy that has the largest (or maximum) minimum payoff. This is called, for obvious reasons, the maximin criterion. By choosing this strategy, we are always guaranteed a payoff of at least the amount given in the table above for that strategy. In this case the maximin criterion would result in our choosing S2, and we would be guaranteed at least a payoff of 1. (In this particular case, it so happens that 1 is also the most we would ever get, but that is an idiosyncrasy of this example.) The choice of any other strategy could result in a payoff of less than this amount. In other words, this criterion is equivalent to saying: Choose your strategy as if the worst is going to happen.

A different criterion was suggested by Leonid Hurwicz. Essentially Hurwicz says, in reference to Wald's criterion: Why should one be a complete pessimist and assume the worst is always going to happen? Why not be an

optimist and assume that the best is going to happen? Or, at least, why not
be partly optimistic? Hurwicz suggests introducing a <u>coefficient of optimism</u>
measured from zero (complete pessimist) to 1 (complete optimist). We can
best illustrate Hurwicz's criterion by first considering the two extremes. We
have already seen the minimum payoffs for each strategy, under Wald's
criterion above. If we were complete optimists, we would choose the strategy
that has the largest possible payoff. We would first make a table showing the
largest payoff for each strategy and then choose the strategy with the largest
value. Thus, the largest possible payoff if we choose S1 is 2; the largest
possible payoff if we choose S2 is 1; etc. We quickly get the following table,
to which we have added the minimum payoff table for comparison:

	Maximum payoff	Minimum payoff
S1	2	0
S2	1	1
S3	4	0
S4	3	0

Clearly, if we were complete optimists, we would choose S3; and if we were
complete pessimists, as we saw before, we would choose S2. Hurwicz suggests that, if we were partially optimistic, we would weight these two values
for each strategy and base our decision criterion on the single value that
would result. Thus, suppose our coefficient of optimism is z. He suggests
calculating for each strategy the quantity: z (maximum payoff) + 1 - z
(minimum payoff). Remember that the coefficient of optimism is, by definition,
between 0 and 1. You will note that setting $z = 1$ leads to using the complete
optimist's criterion, as it should. Similarly, setting $z = 0$ leads to the
criterion of the complete pessimist, Wald's criterion. Suppose we choose an
intermediate value of the coefficient of optimism -- say, $z = 1/2$. Our calculations, together with the resulting value for each strategy, are:

Hurwicz value for $z = 1/2$

S1	$1/2(2) + 1/2(0) =$	1.0
S2	$1/2(1) + 1/2(1) =$	1.0
S3	$1/2(4) + 1/2(0) =$	2.0
S4	$1/2(3) + 1/2(0) =$	1.5

The Hurwicz criterion is that we should choose that strategy with the largest value so calculated. In this case it would lead us to choose S3, assuming that we feel our coefficient of optimism is satisfactorily approximated by $z = 1/2$. It is difficult to verbalize this criterion except by saying that it introduces one's optimism into the decision criterion. If one feels "lucky," this is the way to be rational about it. This method represents an averaging of the extreme outcomes, rather than an average of all -- which is the Laplace criterion.

A fourth criterion was introduced by Leonard J. Savage. Savage says: Suppose we knew in advance the state of nature that was going to occur; then we would certainly choose the strategy that would give us the largest return for that state of nature. Thus, if we knew that N1 was going to occur, we would certainly choose S1 -- since, if N1 occurred, that strategy would give us a larger payoff than any other strategy. Now, suppose that we did not know what state of nature was going to occur and we chose strategy 3 (S3): If N1 did, in fact, occur, we would lose a certain amount because we did not know that N1 was going to occur. Specifically, if we chose S3 and N1 occurred, we would receive a payoff of 0; whereas, as we have seen, we would have received a payoff of 2 if we had chosen S1 and N1 had occurred. Our loss due to our ignorance is measured by the differences between the 2 we could have received and the 0 we did receive, or $2 - 0 = 2$. Savage calls this the measure of our regret at not having chosen the best strategy for the particular state of nature that did occur.

In short, regret is measured by the difference between the payoff one receives and the payoff he could have received if he had known the state of nature in advance. It is clear that there is a unique regret connected with each payoff in the original table. To get the regret associated with each of the payoffs, we need only determine the maximum payoff for each column in the table (each state of nature), and then subtract this value from every other payoff in that column. Thus, the maximum possible payoff in N1 is 2. Subtracting this value from each of the values in the column under N1 gives, respectively, 0, -1, -2, and -1. Proceeding in this way we will get a new table, which will contain nothing but zeros and negative numbers. For our example we get:

	N1	N2	N3	N4
S1	0	-2	-1	0
S2	-1	-3	0	0
S3	-2	0	-1	-1
S4	-1	-1	-1	-1

This is called the regret matrix. Savage's criterion is, now, to use Wald's maximin criterion on this regret matrix. To use the Wald criterion, it will be recalled, it is first necessary to determine the minimum payoff for each strategy. Thus, the minimum payoff for S1 in this regret matrix is -2. Proceeding similarly we get:

	Minimum regret
S1	-2
S2	-3
S3	-2
S4	-1

The Wald criterion is that we should choose the strategy that has the maximum such minimum, the maximin regret in this case. This maximin value of regret is -1, which occurs if we choose S4. This, therefore, according to the Savage criterion, is the strategy we should choose. The choice of this strategy will mean that we will have held our regret to a minimum against the worst that can happen.

We have suggested and illustrated four different decision criteria, and each one of them has led to a different choice of strategy:

Decision criterion	Strategy chosen
Laplace	S1
Wald	S2
Hurwicz	S3
Savage	S4

Of course, the example we used was "cooked" so that each criterion would determine a different strategy. Although this will not always happen, different criteria generally will determine different strategies.

No one of these criteria is "better" than another. They are just different. Other criteria could be suggested, but the criteria illustrated should be enough to demonstrate that there are a number of criteria, each with its own rationale and each logically defensible. The adherent of the Laplace criterion can say: "If you use this criterion over a large number of such decision problems, you will get a greater average payoff than if you use any other criterion." The adherent of the Wald criterion may answer: "That is true, but you can go bankrupt using the Laplace criterion if you get a run of bad luck; whereas, by using the Wald criterion, you always know that you will never do worse than the maximin value." The adherent of the Hurwicz criterion could add his own comments about each of these. To the Laplace adherent he might say, "Since most important decision problems are never repeated, if you don't take advantage of a particular opportunity it may never recur; therefore, the theoretical large number of similar problems is irrelevant." To the Wald adherent he might point out, "There is no need to assume that nature is always conspiring against you. Why not be a little bit optimistic?" Similarly, the adherent of the Savage criterion can present arguments and counterarguments in his favor.

SUMMARY AND CONCLUSIONS

The foregoing review of decision theory indicates that most decisions can be reduced to a series of four steps: (1) The objectives of the decision-maker must be formulated precisely. (2) He must select a "payoff" (a measure of effectiveness or success) in terms of his objectives. (3) He must evaluate the payoff for each possible strategy, granting the conditions that obtain and the resources at his command. (4) He must select among alternative strategies on the basis of alternative decision criteria.

The most important ideas uncovered in the discussion are: It is very helpful to use a payoff matrix (which indicates the payoff for each combination of strategy with a state of nature) as a conceptual device for arriving at decisions. The payoff employed must accurately incorporate the decision-maker's objectives, for otherwise he may maximize his payoff without accomplishing his objectives. Finally, there is no single "best" decision criterion for choosing among alternative strategies.

CHAPTER II

THEORY OF GAMES

The decision problems we will now consider are those in which the state
of nature depends in some way on our choice of strategy. The theoretical
treatment of such decision problems is known as game theory. Analogously,
decision problems such as those we discussed in the preceding chapter are
often called games against nature. Decision problems in which the state of
nature is dependent on the choice of strategy are called "games" because their
clearest prototype is the decision made in a game. In poker, for example, the
gains of one player are achieved at the expense of the other players; and each
player must assume that the other players will choose strategies that will
minimize his gains.

It is unfortunate that this kind of decision theory is called game theory,
for it sounds as if it were of no more import than, say, a book on chess open-
ings. Actually, nothing could be further from the truth. Game theory deals
with decision problems in which the conditions confronting the decision-maker
are influenced by his choice of strategy. It is true that many parlor games fit
this description. So, however, does the fighting of a war, for a military com-
mander must assume his opponent will attempt to frustrate his purpose. Similarly, in oligopolistic markets it can be assumed that one's competitors will
attempt to further their own ends and, in so doing, will come into conflict with
one's own purposes. The choice of a strategy of cutting prices, for example,
might have an excellent payoff if the state of nature were unaffected by the
price cut. However, if one's competitors react by cutting prices even more,
the result may be a considerable loss. These examples should serve to indicate that the theory of games covers a great number of decision problems of the
utmost importance, and that it is by no means trivial or unimportant.

Games can be classified according to the number of opponents, which
can vary from two opponents (two-person game) up to n opponents (n-person
game). Games are further characterized by the degree of conflict of interest
among the opponents. Complete conflict of interest means that the amount one
person gains, and exactly that amount, is lost by his opponents. Games in
which this is true are called zero-sum games, for reasons that will soon become evident. In nonzero-sum games, the conflict of interest is not complete,

so that the amount gained by one person is not necessarily lost by his opponents. Game theory has a large and intricate literature, and we cannot do more than indicate some of the main ideas that have been introduced as a result of the analysis of this sort of decision problem. Consequently, we will have to confine our attention mainly to two-person games; and, even so, we will not be able to deal very extensively with two-person nonzero-sum games.

In some parlor games, the payoff will depend only on the opponents' selections of strategies. In economic "games," however, the payoff will generally depend on the state of nature as well as on the choices of strategy. For example, the payoffs to two firms might depend on their choices of pricing strategies and on a number of factors outside the control of the firms in question -- general economic conditions, shifts in demand, etc. This means that the payoff table needed to describe such a situation would have to include all the possible choices of strategies as well as the possible states of nature. For greater simplicity in our discussion, we will ignore the various states of nature and consider payoff tables that depend only on the choices of strategy. This will suit our purpose, since we are primarily interested in discussing some of the problems of selecting strategies against a rational opponent. The reader should remember, however, that in realistic situations the states of nature that may occur are a necessary part of the payoff table.

Before we begin to discuss some typical games, we should get our terminology clearly fixed. As remarked above, we will no longer be talking about states of nature. Instead, we will be considering our opponent's possible choices of strategy. From the standpoint of procedure, the tabular presentation of the payoffs remains the same: for each possible strategy we might choose, there are a number of possible payoffs. The specific payoff that we, in fact, receive will be determined by the strategy our opponent selects. Thus, our payoff table will have our possible strategies as rows and our opponent's possible strategies as columns. Further, it will no longer be necessary to state the objective in each case. We will assume that the objective is always to get the largest possible return, and that the payoff has been put in units suitable to express this objective. Our main attention then will be devoted to the establishment of decision criteria. It is also worth noting that the difference between zero-sum and nonzero-sum games depends on the payoff table. As will be illustrated below, if we have a zero-sum game, only one table is required to give the payoffs for both players; otherwise, more than one payoff table is required.

Let us fix some of these ideas by constructing the payoff table for a simple game -- the game of Two-Finger Morra, which has been played in Italy since classical antiquity. This game is played by two persons; each player shows one or two fingers and simultaneously calls his guess as to the number of fingers his opponent will show. If just one of the opponents guesses correctly, he wins an amount equal to the sum of the fingers shown by both him and his opponent. Otherwise, the game is a draw. First, let us enumerate the strategies. In this particular game, each opponent has the same possible strategies. He can show either one or two fingers and he can simultaneously call his guess of either one or two. He has, therefore, four possible strategies:

S1: Show one finger and guess one (1, 1).
S2: Show one finger and guess two (1, 2).
S3: Show two fingers and guess one (2, 1).
S4: Show two fingers and guess two (2, 2).

Our payoff table must therefore include four rows and four columns to accommodate all the possible combinations of strategies. Let us now determine the payoffs for the various combinations of strategies. For convenience, we will refer to the two opponents as A and B. Now, suppose A chooses S1: he shows one finger and guesses that his opponent will show one finger. Four possibilities exist, corresponding to the four possible strategies that B might adopt. Suppose B chooses S1. Then both have guessed correctly; and, according to the rules of the game, a draw results, so that the payoff is zero. Suppose B chooses S2 -- that is, he shows one finger and guesses two. Then A has guessed correctly but B has not; and the rules of the game show that A wins the sum of the fingers shown by both A and B, in this case 1 + 1 = 2. The payoff, in short, is 2. If B chooses S3, B has guessed correctly and A has not; so A loses 1 + 2 = 3. In this case the payoff to A is -3, the negative sign indicating that he has lost. If B chooses S4, neither opponent has guessed correctly; and the rules of the game show that the payoff is zero. It is easy to determine similarly the payoffs for the other choices of strategy by A, and the reader may want to verify one of the last three rows in the following table in order to be sure he understands how the table was compiled. The results can be presented in the payoff table:

A's Payoff Table

| | | B's Strategies | | | |
		S1	S2	S3	S4
	S1	0	2	-3	0
	S2	-2	0	0	3
A's Strategies	S3	3	0	0	-4
	S4	0	-3	4	0

What would B's payoff table look like? It is clear that this is a zero-sum game, since whatever A wins B loses, and vice versa. Therefore, we know immediately, without any calculation, that B's table will be precisely the same as this one, with all the signs reversed. Thus, if A chooses S3 and B chooses S4, the payoff to A is, as in the table, -4. This means that A loses four units. Obviously, the corresponding entry in B's table is simply + 4, since B wins four units. In short, for a zero-sum game one <u>payoff matrix</u> or table suffices for both players.[1]

We see, then, that for zero-sum games (of which Two-Finger Morra is an example), we need only one payoff table. This one table completely describes the game. Let us explore the connection between this kind of payoff table and the behavior of the players. The table we have given is the payoff for A, and we can clearly assume that A's objective is to maximize his return from the game. What about B? His objective would also be to maximize his return from the game. However, when we use A's payoff table to describe B's payoffs, as we are doing, we can no longer state B's objective in this way. From B's point of view, all the signs in the payoff table are wrong. Fortunately this introduces no real difficulties. To state B's objective in terms of A's payoff table we merely change from maximums to minimums. B's objective, then, is to minimize the payoff to A -- which he does when the outcome is the largest negative number in the payoff table. Negative results represent payoffs from A to B, which B desires to make as large as possible.

Granted A's and B's objective and using the payoff table as given, let us try to reason our way through to a choice of strategy for A. He might start out by saying that he should use S4 because that strategy would give him a chance of getting a payoff of four units if B chooses S3. But A may then reason that B will expect him to choose S4 and that therefore B will certainly not choose S3; rather, he will choose S2 and cause A to lose three units. So A thinks further and decides that he will not choose S3 but will choose S1, so that he can win two units when B chooses S2. But A must reckon with the possibility that B will suspect this too, and will choose S3 so that A will lose three units. A should then reason that if B is going to choose S3, <u>he</u> should choose S4 and win four units. And we are back where we started! We could reason around this circle indefinitely and never resolve the question. How, then, can we determine a reasonable decision criterion? In order to answer this question, we will have to introduce some of the concepts of game theory. The example given, the simple game of Two-Finger Morra, should suffice to indicate that the determination of a decision criterion is not necessarily a simple matter.

---

[1]This is true only for a zero-sum game or a constant-sum game, of which the zero-sum game is a special case. We shall illustrate the idea of a constant-sum game below. Suffice it for the moment to state that all the essential ideas and concepts of this type of game are conveyed by considering the zero-sum game. The important theoretical distinction arises when we consider those games in which we cannot use one payoff table to represent the payoff of both players.

For our discussion of two-person zero-sum games, we will use some examples that are easier to analyze than Two-Finger Morra. We have already explained that we need only give the payoff table for one player in a two-player zero-sum game. This suffices to describe the game in question completely. Therefore, we will not offer verbal descriptions of all our examples but shall simply refer to the payoff table. We need only know that the two opponents have complete freedom of choice among the various strategies indicated, and that the table indicates the payoff for each pair of possible strategies.

Game 1

Not all games are as difficult as Two-Finger Morra insofar as the determination of a decision criterion is concerned. Some two-person zero-sum games are such that it is completely evident what strategy should be chosen. Consider a game with the following payoff table (A's payoff):

		B's Strategies	
		S1	S2
A's	S1	1	3
Strategies	S2	-3	-1

We will follow the convention of always using rows to represent A's possible strategies and columns for B's possible strategies. A wants to maximize his return, as usual. It is immediately clear that he will always choose S1. Why? Because S1 always gives him a greater return than S2, no matter what B does. B wants to minimize the payoff to A, also as usual. It is clear that B will always choose his strategy S1. Why? Because A's payoff is less when B uses his strategy S1 than when he uses S2, no matter what A does. Our conclusion is, then, that both opponents will always choose their S1 strategy, and the payoff will always be one unit to A.

This game illustrates the concept of dominance. We say that, for A, one strategy dominates another if every payoff in that strategy is greater than or equal to the corresponding payoff in the other strategy. In the present example, S1 dominates S2 because 1 is greater than -3 and 3 is greater than -1. For B we say that one strategy dominates another if every payoff in the first strategy is less than or equal to the corresponding payoff for the second strategy. For B, S1 dominates S2 because 1 is less than 3 and -3 is less than -1. It is never to a player's advantage to use a dominated strategy.

We have seen that this game will always result in a payoff to A of one unit.

This game then has a value of 1 to A or -- what amounts to the same thing -- a value of -1 to B. Thus, if the players adhere to their best strategies -- which we have just determined to be S1 for each of them -- then A will win one unit each time the game is played. Why can we say that these are the best strategies? Consider what will happen if one of the players diverges from this strategy (S1). Suppose, for example, that A chooses his second strategy (S2). Then, assuming B has used S1, A will lose three units instead of winning one unit as he could have. Similarly, if B uses S2 instead of S1, then A will gain (B will lose) three units instead of the one unit to which B could have held A by selecting S1. In other words, if the players diverge from their best strategy in this game, they will do worse than if they adhere to S1. Therefore, we are justified in saying that S1 is the best strategy for each player.

Game 2

Let us consider another simple example. Consider the game with the following payoff table for A:

	S1	S2	S3	S4
S1	6	-3	15	-11
S2	7	1	9	5
S3	-3	0	-5	8

This game serves to illustrate that the two players need not have the same number of strategies. Note that we are still following the convention of using the rows for A's possible strategies and the columns for B's possible strategies. We wish to determine decision criteria for both A and B to use in choosing their strategies. One approach, which might suggest itself as a result of the previous discussion of the general decision problem, is to use the Wald minimax or maximin criterion. Thus, A might reason that if he chooses S1, he might lose as much as -11; if he chooses S3, he might lose as much as -5; but if he chooses S2, the worst that can happen is that he wins 1. In short, we have a minimum payoff for each row of the payoff table, which is the same thing as the minimum payoff for each of A's possible strategies:

	Row minimum
S1	-11
S2	1
S3	-5

If we use the Wald criterion, we must, it will be remembered, choose the strategy with the largest such minimum value. We call this value the maximin value. In this case the maximin value is 1, and the criterion establishes that we should choose S2. By so doing we will maximize our payoff against the worst possible occurrences.

Let us use the same criterion on B's strategies. Recall that the payoffs are given in A's terms. B wants to minimize the payoff to A, which is the same thing as maximizing his own payoff. What is the worst possible outcome for B for a particular strategy? Clearly, it is the largest payoff in the corresponding column, since this is the largest amount B might lose to A if B adopts that strategy. Thus, if B chooses his S1, the worst he can do is to lose 7 -- which will happen if A chooses S2. Any other choice by A will result in a smaller loss for B if B has chosen S1. Thus, the maximum payoffs for each column represent the worst that B can do for each of his possible strategies:

	Column maximum
S1	7
S2	1
S3	15
S4	8

Using the Wald criterion for B requires that B should select the strategy that has the minimum such maximum value, called the minimax value. In this case the minimax value is 1, for S2. Therefore, the Wald criterion dictates that B should choose S2. By so doing B will minimize the payoff to A (maximize his own payoff) against the worst possible occurrences.

When we dealt with the Wald criterion in the general decision problems, which we called games against nature, it was only one possible criterion among a number of equally reasonable criteria. In games against rational opponents, as here, the situation is entirely different. We can now make an extremely plausible case that the only reasonable criterion is the Wald criterion -- simply because one's opponent is presumably behaving rationally in such a manner as to achieve the best possible payoff for himself; and, at least in zero-sum games, there is a direct and complete conflict of interests. Let us follow out the reasoning. If A chooses S2, then B will lose more than 1 if he chooses any strategy other than S2. Therefore, since B desires to minimize A's payoff, he is forced to choose S2. Similarly, if B chooses S2, then A will receive a payoff of less than 1 if he chooses any strategy other than S2. Since A wishes to maximize his payoff, he is forced to choose S2. Thus, the fact that the opponents are rational, and that each wishes to achieve the maximum possible payoff for himself, leads directly to the use of the Wald criterion. Any other choice of strategy will result in a smaller payoff for the player using it.

It is important to emphasize this distinction between games against nature and games against rational opponents. In games against nature the player has a choice of a number of possible decision criteria, no one of which can be demonstrated to be "best" -- since the state of nature that occurs is independent of the decion-maker's choice of strategy. In games against rational opponents this is no longer the case. The objective of maximizing returns can be achieved only by following the Wald criterion.

One feature of the game we are considering makes it particularly easy to analyze. In our utilization of the Wald criterion, we determined, for A, the maximin value for rows and, for B, the minimax value for columns. It will be noted that, in the present example, these two values are equal -- both of them being 1. When this is true of a game, there are two particularly important implications. First, when the row maximin value equals the column minimax value, it follows that each player must use a specific strategy to achieve the maximum possible payoff. In other words, this equality of maximin and minimax guarantees that the utilization of the Wald criterion by each player will result in the selection of a unique strategy for that player. In our example this equality resulted in there being one best strategy for A -- namely, S2 -- and one best strategy for B -- also S2. Second, when the minimax equals the maximin, the value of the game is the same as the value of the minimax (and the maximin). In our example, this value is 1; therefore, the value of the game, to A, is 1. This means that if A follows his best strategy, S2, he is assured of a payoff of at least 1 for each play of the game. The value of the game to B is, of course, -1, with a similar interpretation.

MIXED STRATEGIES

By using the method that we followed in our last example, we can easily determine whether a game has this equality between minimax and maximin. When this equality exists, the analysis of the game is complete: the best strategies for the two players are determined by the row and column that have this minimax value at their intersection, and the value of the game is equal to the minimax (or maximin) value. This constitutes the complete answer to the decision problem presented by the game. Unfortunately, for many games the minimax does not equal the maximin, and the analysis of these games is more difficult. We must now consider methods for determining strategies in games for which the row maximin does not equal the column minimax.

As an example of such a game, we may take Two-Finger Morra. The pay-off table (for A) of this game was given above. For convenience we repeat it here:

	S1	S2	S3	S4
S1	0	2	-3	0
S2	-2	0	0	3
S3	3	0	0	-4
S4	0	-3	4	0

Suppose we proceed as before and determine the various row minimums and column maximums:

Row minimum		Column maximum	
S1	-3	S1	3
S2	-2	S2	2
S3	-4	S3	4
S4	-3	S4	3

The maximum of the row minimums (the maximin value) is -2. The minimum of the column maximums (the minimax value) is 2. Clearly, the maximin does not equal the minimax in this game. Consequently, it is not obvious what strage-gies the players should use. If A chooses S2 and B chooses S2, the payoff will be zero. But if B thinks that A will choose S2, then B will choose S1 and A will lose two units. If A anticipates this choice of S1 by B, then A will choose S3 and win three units. But if B anticipates the choice of S3 by A, then B will choose S4 and A will lose four units. So we are back in one of those circular arguments, which never resolve the problem of determining what strat-egy to choose. We must go deeper into this problem in order to find a solution.

We can anticipate one major feature of any solution to the problem of determining the best strategies for the players in this game, or in any other game that does not have the minimax equal to the maximin. In Game 2, for which the minimax equaled the maximin, we found that each player had a spe-cific best strategy to follow. The fact that B, for example, knew that A was going to use his strategy S2 made no difference to B in selecting his own strategy. Despite this knowledge he could do no better than to select S2 himself. The same thing, of course, can be said for A. In short, if a player used his best strategy, then the knowledge of this fact did not help his opponent. This is generally true of all games with their minimax equal to their maximin.

This is clearly not true of Two-Finger Morra. Consider A's possible strategies: for each of them there is one positive payoff and one negative payoff. Therefore, if B knew that A was going to use any one of his possible strategies, then B could choose his own strategy so that A would get a negative payoff (suffer a loss). Analogous remarks apply for B, since there is one positive and one negative payoff in each of the columns also. We can certainly conclude, then, that neither of the players can afford to have his rival know the strategy he is employing, if there are repeated plays of the game.

Our first conclusion, then, is that each player will have to use more than one of his strategies in repeated plays of the game. Further, since a player cannot permit his opponent to know in advance what his strategy will be (else he will certainly suffer a loss), it follows that the player cannot use a fixed pattern of choices of his strategies over repeated plays of the game. This means that the best strategy to be followed by either of the players must consist of some kind of random or unexpected selection from his possible strategies. In game theory this sort of strategy is called a _mixed strategy_; in contrast, one specific strategy used throughout any number of plays (as in games 1 and 2) is called a _pure strategy_. A mixed strategy, then, must consist of the random selection of a strategy for each play of the game. Note that we did not say that the player must randomly select a strategy from among _all_ his possible strategies. This remains to be seen. We must attempt to find such a mixed strategy for Two-Finger Morra.

Let us be completely clear concerning that which we want to determine. For the game considered above, where the row maximin equaled the column minimax, we found that a specific best strategy existed for each of the opponents. If each of the opponents followed his best strategy, then each play of the game would result in a specific payoff, which we called the value of the game. If A did not follow his best strategy, he would get a smaller payoff than the value of the game -- provided B followed his best strategy. A similar statement holds for B. However, for games in which the minimax does not equal the maximin, we know that there is no pure strategy that can be followed by the opponents. Instead, each opponent must use a mixed strategy, which will consist of the random selection of one of his pure strategies with some definite probability. We want to find, for each opponent, the mixed strategy that will give him the maximum payoff. This will enable us to determine the value of the game as well. It is not at all obvious that there must be a best strategy for the opponents in the sense we are considering. However, the so-called _fundamental theorem of game theory_, first proved by Von Neumann, guarantees that this is the case. So we know that best mixed strategies exist -- it remains to find a method for determining them.

Game 4

It will be convenient to illustrate the procedure on a game with a smaller payoff table. Suppose we have the following payoff table (for A):

	S1	S2
S1	3	-2
S2	-4	2

The reader can easily verify that the maximin of the rows is -2 and the minimax of the columns is 2. We know, therefore, that the best strategies for the players will be mixed strategies. Note that we do not know the <u>value</u> of this game: since the value of the game is the payoff to be expected if the best strategies are adopted, we cannot determine the value of the game until we know the best strategies. Or, more precisely, the value of the game and the best strategies must be determined simultaneously. We need some algebra to obtain the desired solution to this decision problem, but the procedure for setting up the equations is clear if we are first completely certain of what we are looking for. A mixed strategy for A will consist of the proportion with which his various possible strategies should be chosen, considering that the game is being repeatedly played. Perhaps, for instance, A should choose S1 65% of the time and S2 35% of the time. Since we know that A must conceal his strategies, we can equally well say that we want to know the <u>probabilities</u> with which he should select his various strategies -- for example, that he should select S1 with a probability of 0.65 and S2 with a probability of 0.35. In short, we want to know what probabilities will constitute the <u>best</u> such choice for A. When we say "best," we mean that the average payoff that A will receive by following this strategy will be as large as or larger than he would get from any other strategy. The <u>average payoff</u> he gets from this best strategy is, therefore, the <u>value of the game</u> to A. Similarly, we want to know the probabilities with which B should select <u>his</u> possible strategies. B's "best" mixed strategy will give a smaller payoff to A than any other strategy B could adopt. This <u>smallest average payoff</u> to A is the <u>value of the game</u> to B. The fundamental theorem, referred to above, guarantees that there is a unique value for any such game. Specifically, the best strategies of A and of B will result in a definite value for the game, and neither A nor B can improve his return if the opponent adheres to his best strategy.

To set up the equations that will give us the best strategies, it is necessary to use some mathematical notation. Let:

v = value of game to A
x = probability that A chooses S1
y = probability that A chooses S2
a = probability that B chooses S1
b = probability that B chooses S2

We know that $x + y = 1$, since A must choose one of his strategies. Similarly, we know that $a + b = 1$. We also know that when A uses his best strategy he must get a return of at least the value of the game (v), no matter what B does. Specifically, therefore, we can say that A, using his best strategy, will get a return of at least v if B always uses S1 or if B always uses S2. Suppose B always uses S1. What will be A's expected return? With a probability of x (as often as A uses S1) he will get a payoff of 3, and with a probability of y (as often as A uses S2) he will get a payoff of -4. A's expected return, then, if B always uses S1, is $3x - 4y$. We know that this must be at least equal to, and perhaps greater than, v. We can therefore immediately write one equation: $3x - 4y \geq v$. Suppose B always uses S2. Then A's expected return will be $-2x + 2y$, which must also be greater than or equal to v. This gives us a second equation: $-2x + 2y \geq v$.

We can now use similar reasoning on B. When B uses his best strategy, he holds the payoff to A (v) down to a minimum. No matter what strategy A adopts, his payoff will be less than or equal to v, if B adheres to his best strategy. Therefore, in particular, this must be true if A adopts either S1 or S2 all the time. Suppose A adopts S1 all the time. Then B would expect the average payoff to A to be less than or equal to v. But if A adopts S1, then he would receive a payoff of 3 with a probability of a (as often as B uses S1) and a payoff of -2 with a probability of b (as often as B uses S2). Therefore, the expected payoff to A in this case is $3a - 2b \leq v$. Similarly, if A adopts S2 all the time, his expected payoff will be $-4a + 2b \leq v$. We now have six equations:

$x + y = 1$	$3x - 4y \geq v$	$3a - 2b \leq v$
$a + b = 1$	$-2x + 2y \geq v$	$-4a + 2b \leq v$

Four of these equations are not the usual equalities, with which the reader is probably more or less familiar, but are inequalities. It will be noted that there are only five unknowns: a, b, x, y, and v. It must be remembered that there is an additional set of constraints on the possible solutions, since a, b, x, and y must all be greater than or equal to zero; none of them can be less than zero because we can attach no meaning to a negative probability.

We cannot here undertake a presentation of the theory of solving such sets of equations. Suffice it to say that the first procedure is to try to solve the whole set as if all the equations were equalities. If this can be done, the problem is solved. If it cannot be done, then one of the variables is set equal to zero and the equations are attempted again. This process continues until a solution is achieved. The fundamental theorem of game theory guarantees that we will reach a solution by this method, but it may be computationally onerous.[2]

Let us illustrate the procedure for this example. We start by assuming that all of the inequations are equations:

$$x + y = 1 \qquad\qquad 3x - 4y = v \qquad\qquad 3a - 2b = v$$

$$a + b = 1 \qquad\qquad -2x + 2y = v \qquad\qquad -4a + 2b = v$$

We substitute $y = 1 - x$ and $b = 1 - a$ in the other four equations and get, after simplifying,

$$7x - 4 = v \qquad\qquad 5a - 2 = v$$

$$-4x + 2 = v \qquad\qquad -6a + 2 = v$$

From the first two equations we easily determine that $v = -2/11$ and $x = 6/11$. Note that if x had been less than zero we would know that we had to start over again by setting one of the variables equal to zero (not necessarily x). It may now turn out that this value of v does not permit us to determine a. In this event we would also have to start over. However, in the present case we find that $a = 4/11$ satisfies both of the equations containing a. Our problem is therefore solved. The complete solution is:

$$x = 6/11 \qquad\qquad a = 4/11 \qquad\qquad v = -2/11$$

$$y = 5/11 \qquad\qquad b = 7/11$$

We can therefore summarize the best mixed strategy for A and for B as follows:

A's best mixed strategy: Choose randomly between S1 with probability of 6/11 and S2 with probability of 5/11.

B's best mixed strategy: Choose randomly between S1 with probability of 4/11 and S2 with probability of 7/11.

Value of Game: -2/11 (On the average, A will lose 2/11 each time the game is played.)

As long as either player adheres to his best strategy, his opponent cannot increase his payoff above the value of the game. The reader should verify this

---

[2]For details, the interested reader is referred to J. C. C. McKinsey, Introduction to the Theory of Games (New York: McGraw-Hill Book Co., 1952).

by determining what will happen if A uses his best strategy, as above, and B uses a pure strategy -- only one of his two strategies.

Let us return now to our example of Two-Finger Morra (Game 3). We do not propose to carry out the details of the solution to determine the optimal strategies. Suffice it to say that, as might be expected, the value of this game is zero and both of the players have the same optimal strategy: randomly to select S2 with probability of 3/5 and S3 with probability of 2/5. Neither S1 nor S4 is used in the optimal strategy. We do not recommend to the reader that he should attempt to calculate this optimal strategy. Actually, this particular example is interesting in another way. There is, for each player, an infinity of strategies that guarantee him the expected value of the game. Precisely, either player can choose any probability between 4/7 and 3/5 for choosing S2 or, correspondingly, any probability between 3/7 and 2/5 for choosing S3. Naturally, a player's choice of one of the two probabilities also determines his other choice, because the two must sum to 1. Any one of this infinity of possible mixed strategies will guarantee the player at least a return of zero. The reader can verify for himself that the specific mixed strategy given above (choosing S2 with probability of 3/5) will give the largest return if the player's opponent diverges from his optimal strategy. In short, there is an infinity of strategies that are optimal in the sense that they guarantee the player a payoff equal to the value of the game to him. From among this infinity of strategies, that particular one is called best which will give the largest payoff to the player if his opponent diverges from his optimal strategy.

SUMMARY AND CONCLUSIONS

Following are some of the important ideas and concepts that we have tried to illustrate in our discussion of the two-person zero-sum game.

First: The conflict of interests between the opponents, and the presumed rationality of the opponents, leads directly to the use of the Wald minimax criterion for choosing strategies.

Second: The fundamental theorem of game theory shows that each of these games does have a unique value and strategies that will achieve this value for each player. The optimal strategies will sometimes be pure strategies, in which case each player should choose a _specific one_ of his strategies. In other cases a mixed strategy is required; and the player must select randomly, with certain given probabilities, the particular strategy he uses. The distinction between the two cases is equivalent to whether the game does or does not have the maximin of the rows equal to the minimax of the columns.

Finally: The determination of the optimal mixed strategy can be quite arduous. Even in some very simple games, the best mixed strategies frequently are not at all obvious.

CHAPTER III

PRICING IN COMPETITIVE BIDDING[1]

Competitive bidding is one kind of pricing. It calls for each firm bidding on a particular contract to submit a sealed bid; the firm that submits the lowest bid, or price, is awarded the contract. This is a perfectly realistic and extremely illuminating kind of pricing problem, although relatively few firms face it directly.

How should a firm determine price when engaged in competitive bidding? What would constitute an optimal pricing policy? We will consider here some of the answers to these questions that have been suggested in recent work in operations research.

The best strategy for a firm to follow -- we shall call it a pricing policy -- depends largely upon the objective of the firm. We can evaluate different business policies or strategies only by considering the degree to which they contribute to the firm's objectives. Any one of a considerable number of completely reasonable objectives might motivate a particular firm at a particular time. Here are some possibilities:

1. Maximize immediate profit.

2. Maximize long-run profit.

3. Obtain a given return on investment.

4. Minimize profits of competitors.

5. Minimize risk of excessive losses.

6. Obtain a greater share of the market.

7. Strengthen the position of management.

---

[1]The analysis of competitive bidding presented in this chapter is derived from Lawrence Friedman, "A Competitive Bidding Strategy," Operations Research, Feb. 1956.

In this discussion we will assume that the firm pursues only the first of these objectives, the maximization of immediate profits. This is certainly a common objective (it is the one assumed in price theory), and it is also amenable to the methods we are going to use. We note explicitly, however, that if a firm maintains a different objective, it might require a different pricing policy than the one we are going to develop.

Since the objective of the firm on which our analysis will be based is to maximize its immediate profit, we must ask: What do we mean by "immediate profit" in this type of situation? Consider a firm that submits a bid on a contract. If the firm is awarded the contract, it will cost the firm a certain amount to fulfill its contractual obligations. The firm's profit will be the difference between the bid and the cost to the firm. This is what we mean by the firm's immediate profit. We can write this symbolically. Let:

x = amount of bid

c = cost of fulfilling obligations under contract

Then, $x - c$ = immediate profit to the firm

This figure may, of course, be negative -- in which case the firm has suffered a loss. We have ignored the cost of making the bid, partly for purposes of simplicity. However, since bidding costs are "sunk costs," which are not affected by whether or not the firm wins the contract, it is not unreasonable to ignore them.

We have offered an unambiguous statement of what we mean by immediate profit; but, unfortunately, there is a vital qualification in our verbal statement, which was not taken into account in our symbolic representation. The culprit is the seemingly innocuous word "if" in the phrase "if the firm is awarded the contract." The presence of this word will lead us to introduce a new concept and to revise our phrasing of the firm's objective. Why does this "if" have such an effect on our formulation of the problem?

The "if" simply expresses the fact that one will not know the result of any particular bid. It is clear that after the contract has been awarded one of two things will have occurred: either the firm got the contract for its bid of x and will make a profit of $x - c$, or it did not get the contract -- in which case its profit will be zero. But what can we say about the profit on a particular contract before the firm makes its bid on that contract? We cannot say that the profit will be $x - c$, because it may be zero. Correspondingly, we cannot say that the profit will be zero, because it might be $x - c$. This basic uncertainty about results is at the heart of our whole problem -- and is involved in almost every business decision.

A specialized branch of study has been developed to deal with uncertainties such as these. Put in a complicated nutshell, it is based on the use of probabilities to express degrees of uncertainty. It should occasion no surprise that we must here introduce the concept of expected profits, and that this concept comes from probability theory. The concept is a fairly simple one, but its importance requires that it should be understood thoroughly; we will therefore devote the next few paragraphs to an explanation of it.

Let us accordingly try to understand precisely how probabilities are measures of uncertainty. What do we mean when we say that the probability of a coin's showing heads on a toss is 1/2? Or that the probability of a person's rolling a seven with a pair of dice is 1/6? Or that the probability of a person's being dealt a perfect hand in bridge (13 cards of the same suit) is 1/158,758,389,900? In any of these cases, the event in question could either happen or not. What information does the associated probability give us? The probability tells us only how likely it is that the given event will occur. Will it occur on the first "trial"? The coin may show tails on the first try or on the first two tries -- or on the first ten tries. We can say only that the proportion of heads will be close to 1/2 if we toss the coin a sufficient number of times. Therefore, we say that the probability (of 1/2 in the preceding example) gives us the proportion of the trials in which we can expect the event to occur in the long run, or on the average. We might deal bridge hands 158,758,389,900 times and never get a perfect hand, or we might (conceivably) get one on the first deal. Probability theory tells us, however, that if we dealt out an enormous number of hands -- perhaps one bridge hand for every electron and proton in the universe (15,747,724,136,275,002,577,605,653,961,181,555,468,044, 717,914,527,116,709,366,231,425,076,185,631,031,296 times 2, according to Sir Arthur S. Eddington) -- we would find that we had gotten pretty nearly one perfect hand for every 158,758,389,900 deals.

Now, in many kinds of situations -- coin tosses and card hands are familiar examples -- it so happens that we are able to calculate probabilities "in advance." But this is, from our present point of view, a coincidence. Suppose we are told that the probability is 1/10 that the average January temperature in New York City will be greater than 40 degrees. What does this mean? It means, first, that someone has gone over the New York City weather records and has discovered that, in the past, one out of ten Januaries had an average temperature of more than 40 degrees. It also means that, barring major climatological changes, we can expect approximately the same proportion in the future. At least this is the best information we have concerning the proportion to be expected in the future. Note that the difference between this case and those above has to do only with the method of determining the probabilities, not their interpretation. If we don't know how to calculate the probability of getting a seven with one roll of a pair of dice, we can roll the dice a great many times and observe the frequency with which we get a seven. As a matter of fact, this is precisely how it was done, and with considerable accuracy, by all gamblers before probability theory was developed in the seventeenth century.

The meaning of a probability, then, is that it gives the relative frequency with which we can expect an event to occur in the long run, or on the average. If we toss a coin 100 times, we can expect to get about $1/2(100) = 50$ heads. If we roll dice 600 times, we can expect to get about $1/6(600) = 100$ sevens. If we know that the probability of a bad loan is $3/70$, then, out of 210 loans, we can expect $3/70(210) = 9$ bad ones. Let us consider how the foregoing might be useful in dealing with possible profits and losses.

Suppose you have the choice of making two investments of \$1,000. Suppose the return on investment A will be $4\frac{1}{2}\%$ and the return on investment B will be 6%. Granted the certainty of these statements, and assuming that you are motivated by the objective of getting the greatest possible return, you will undoubtedly invest in B. This conclusion follows because your return from B will be \$60 and your return from A will be only \$45. But suppose you are in-formed that the probability of a return on A is 0.9 and the probability of a return on B is 0.65. (We assume that either the returns are the given percen-tages, or else there is no return at all.) How would you choose between the investments?

We could reason as follows about B. The meaning of the probability of 0.65 is that, if we could repeat an investment in B 100 times, we would ex-pect to have about 65 of our investments give us a return of \$60. In the other 35 investments, we would get a return of zero. Therefore, the average return per investment would be, for all 100,

$$\frac{65(\$60) + 35(\$0)}{100} = \$39.00.$$

This, then, is the return we could expect, on the average, and is called the expected return on B. Analogously, for A we would expect that out of 100 in-vestments we would get returns on about $0.9(100) = 90$. For these 90 we would get a return of \$45 each, and for the other 10 we would get no return. Therefore, our average expected return per investment for A would be

$$\frac{90(\$45) + 10(\$0)}{100} = \$40.50.$$

We could now conclude that you should invest in A because your ex-pected return from A is larger than it is from B. If you had the chance to make a series of such investments, you would get, on the average, larger returns by investing in A.

Note that we said "could now conclude" instead of "must now conclude." The reasoning we followed is perfectly logical and affords complete justifica-tion for choosing investment A. However, it is clear that one might prefer, for example, to play a hunch and invest in B, and that he might be right and we might be wrong. This in no way changes the fact that our reasoning is impeccable, granting the probabilities as given and the objective as stated. The same question arises concerning gambling. One person may play the odds correctly and lose, while another ignores them completely and wins. Perhaps some individuals are gifted with a sixth sense. Those of us who do not have such a sixth sense can console ourselves with the fact that most individuals who ignore the relevant probabilities eventually suffer the consequence.

Let us return to our example. It is not necessary to go through the whole chain of reasoning in order to use this idea of expected returns. The expected returns can be easily calculated directly from the returns and the probabilities, without introducing the hypothetical 100 tries (or any other number). Thus, for A we can reason directly: With probability of 0.90, we will get a return of $45; and with probability of 0.1, (i.e., 1 - 0.90), we will get a return of $0. Therefore, our expected return is 0.90($45) + 0.10($0) = $40.50. Similarly, for B we will get a return of $60 with probability of 0.65, and a return of $0 with probability 0.35 (i.e., 1 - 0.65). Our expected return from B is, therefore, 0.65($60) + 0.35($0) = $39.00. This calculation is completely equivalent to the preceding one, but it does not display the logic so clearly. Once the logic is understood, the simpler calculation should be used.

This approach can readily be extended to cases where there are more than two possible returns. Suppose we have two possible courses of action, A and B, with the following possible returns and corresponding probabilities:

A		B	
Return	Probability	Return	Probability
$2,000	0.5	$3,500	0.4
600	.2	400	.3
-500	.3	-2,000	.3

Assuming an objective of maximizing return, which course of action should we choose? The interpretation of the tables should be clear. The only new feature is that there is a probability of loss in each case, as well as the two probabilities of gain. We reason exactly as before. A can produce a return of 2,000 with a probability of 0.5, a return of $600 with a probability of 0.2, and a loss of $500 with a probability of 0.3. The expected return is, then,

0.5($2,000) + 0.2($600) + 0.3(-$500) = $1,000 + $120 - $150 = $970.

Similarly, for B we have an expected return of

0.4($3,500) + 0.3($400) + 0.3(-$2,000) = $1,400 + $120 - $600 = $920.

Since the expected return from A is greater than that from B, we conclude that we should select A.

The relevance of probability theory to competitive bidding should be obvious. Generally, for a given contract, the higher the bid, the less the probability of the bidder's being awarded the contract. We can readily take this fact into account by using the notion of expected profit from a contract. Suppose, for example, that for a particular contract c = $20,000. Suppose also that the firm knows that a bid (x) of $40,000 has a probability of 0.3, and that a bid of $30,000 has a probability of 0.7 of being awarded the contract. Which of these two bids should it make? We reason as follows: If it is awarded the contract, its profit on a bid of $40,000 will be $40,000 - $20,000 = $20,000; its profit on a bid of $30,000 will be $10,000. If the bid is $40,000, there could be a return of $20,000 with a probability of 0.3, or a return of $0 with a probability of 0.7 (i.e., 1 - 0.3). Therefore, the expected profit on a bid of $40,000 is 0.3($20,000 + 0.7($0) = $6,000. For the bid of $30,000, the expected profit is 0.7($10,000) + 0.3($0) = $7,000.

Since the bid of $30,000 has the larger expected profit, it is the bid that should be submitted.

This concept of expected profit must be used in our formulation of the problem of competitive bidding. For this reason we change the statement of the objective from "maximize immediate profit" to "maximize expected immediate profit." This change in the wording will serve to emphasize the necessity for introducing the idea of probabilities of being awarded the contract. It also states precisely what we intend to do.

Let us now state this concept in terms of the notations we introduced earlier. If the firm is awarded the contract, it will make a profit of x - c. If it is not awarded the contract, it will make a profit of zero. Suppose that we know the probability of the firm's being awarded the contract for its bid of x. Let this probability be p. Since the firm will either be awarded the contract or not, it follows that the probability of its not being awarded the contract is simply 1 - p. Therefore, with a probability of p the firm will be awarded the contract for its bid of x and will make a profit of x - c. With a probability of 1 - p the firm will not be awarded the contract and will make a profit of zero. Exactly as before, we can now write the expression for the firm's expected profit:

$$\text{Expected profit} = p(x - c) + (1 - p)(0) = p(x - c)$$

since, of course, $(1 - p)(0) = 0$. Let us state once more the meaning of this expected profit. The expected profit represents the average return per bid which the firm could expect if (1) it repeated the same bid on a large number of contracts with precisely the same cost and (2) the probability of its being awarded the contract remained fixed at p.

All of this so far has simply been a definition of what we mean by "expected profit," which we have stated the firm is trying to maximize. It is clear that expected profit can be calculated if we know the probability of the firm's being awarded the contract for a given bid. Our first step toward the reality of the situation with which we are dealing comes when we note that the probability of being awarded the contract is related to the size of the bid. This is obvious since, on the one hand, a firm could certainly make such a high bid on a contract that the probability of its being awarded the contract would be zero; and, on the other hand, a firm could make a bid so low (zero, for example) that it would be virtually certain to be awarded the contract. (In this last case, we would say that the probability of its being awarded the contract for that bid is 1.) This means that the probability of award varies with -- is a function of -- the size of the bid. For a given contract, the higher the bid, the less the probability of the bidder's being awarded the contract -- although other factors might affect the outcome. In short, there is some relationship between probability of award and size of bid. This sort of relationship can be expressed as a <u>probability distribution function</u>.

Our purposes require no acquaintance with anything more than the basic nature of such distribution functions. Suppose that all the necessary information was available, and the relationship between the probability of award and the size of bid was known. How might this relationship be presented? What would it look like?

Let us take an example. Assume that a firm is bidding on a contract that will cost $8,000 to complete. For simplicity we will assume that all bids on this contract must be in thousand-dollar units. The relationship between the probability of award and the size of the bid might be presented thus:

Bid x	Probability of award p
$7,000	1.00
8,000	.95
9,000	.85
10,000	.60
11,000	.30
12,000	.10
13,000	.00

This is an example of a probability distribution function. For each allowable bid, there is a given probability of a firm's being awarded the contract if that bid is made. This probability gets smaller as the bid gets larger -- as it should. An actual distribution, to be useful, would give probabilities of award for smaller intervals of the size of bid than we have done, but the principle would be the same. The table indicates that a bid of $7,000 would certainly win the contract but that a bid of $8,000 has a probability of only 0.95 of winning the contract. Why? Because there is a probability of 1.00 - 0.95 = 0.05 that there would be a competitive bid of $7,000, which would beat the bid of $8,000. Similarly, the probability of award at $9,000 goes down to 0.85 because there is a probability of 0.95 - 0.85 = 0.10 of a competitive bid of $8,000. We can continue in this way and determine, by successive subtractions, the probability of each bid, as implied by the above distribution function. We get:

Bid	Probability of bid
$7,000	0.05
8,000	.10
9,000	.25
10,000	.30
11,000	.20
12,000	.10
13,000	.00

This sort of presentation is called a _probability density function_. The sum of the probabilities is 1, since one of these bids must occur and therefore no other is possible. The intimate relationship between distribution functions and their corresponding density functions is obvious: given one of them, the other can be immediately deduced. They simply represent two different ways of presenting the same information. Sometimes one is more useful, sometimes the other.

We have not yet given even a hint as to how a firm might have obtained this distribution function; but let us continue to assume that, somehow, the firm does have it. Given this information, we are able to calculate the expected profit for any bid. We will ignore the possibility of "ties" (equal bids): they do not affect the principle involved; and, because of the large interval of bids we used in presenting our tables, the possibility of ties looks more serious here than it would usually be. Consider a bid of $9,000. If the firm is awarded the contract for this bid, it will make $9,000 - $8,000 = $1,000 profit. This corresponds to the $x - c$ we used above. Since we now know that the probability of the firm's being awarded the contract for this bid is 0.85, we can calculate the expected profit exactly as we did above. Our equation given above was

$$\text{Expected profit} = p(x - c).$$

For the $9,000 bid, we therefore have an expected profit of $0.85(\$9,000 - \$8,000) = \$850$.

Proceeding similarly, we can calculate the expected profit for each bid:

Bid	Expected profit
$7,000	$1.00(\$\ 7,000 - \$8,000) = -\$1,000$
8,000	$.95(\$\ 8,000 - \$8,000) = \qquad 0$
9,000	$.85(\$\ 9,000 - \$8,000) = \qquad 850$
10,000	$.60(\$10,000 - \$8,000) = \quad 1,200$
11,000	$.30(\$11,000 - \$8,000) = \qquad 900$
12,000	$.10(\$12,000 - \$8,000) = \qquad 400$
13,000	$.00(\$13,000 - \$8,000) = \qquad 0$

The maximum expected profit is $1,200, from a bid of $10,000. This, therefore, is the bid the firm should make. Why? Because the firm has the stated objective of maximizing its expected profit, and this bid -- if repeated a large number of times under identical circumstances -- would give the firm an average return of $1,200 per bid, greater than that from any other bid.

We have not yet mentioned one additional assumption in our calculations: that is, we have assumed that the cost of fulfilling the contractual obligations was known (in our example, $8,000). What effect does the undoubted fact that a firm does not know the exact cost have on our reasoning? None. The procedure, and the bid, would remain the same despite any uncertainty about the actual cost. A firm can, and should, accumulate information on the relationship between its estimates and the actual costs of the contracts it has been awarded. This can be done most conveniently by recording, for each completed contract, the ratio between the estimated cost (on which the bid was based) and the actual final cost. By this means, a distribution of these ratios can be obtained, which will be useful in many calculations concerning a firm's over-all position. However, it will have no effect on the bid, as long as there is no bias in the estimation of costs. By bias we mean any long-term tendency for cost estimates to be higher or lower than the actual costs -- for example, 20% too low. Any bias must be corrected or compensated. Granted no bias, then any errors of estimation will have no effect on the bid, since the actual cost is not affected by the bid. Suppose, in our example, the firm's records showed that, for an estimated cost of $8,000, the actual cost could be anywhere between $6,500 and $9,500. This would mean that the actual amount of profit on a contract awarded for a particular bid could range from $1,500 below to $1,500 above the expected profit for that bid. But all the expected profits would be affected equally; therefore, our conclusion that the $10,000 bid will give the maximum expected profit is in no way changed. Therefore, the effect of uncertainty about the cost is to increase the variability of actual profits, but without affecting the relative advantages of the various bids.

The substance of our discussion so far is, then, that it is possible for a firm to determine that bid which will maximize its expected profit. We have outlined a procedure for accomplishing this. In order to utilize our procedure, the firm needs to know only the distribution of probabilities of award as a function of the amount of the bid. But we can very well say at this point, with Hamlet: "Aye, there's the rub!" How can a firm know this distribution? This is the heart of the problem, and the rest of our remarks will be directed toward indicating how this distribution might be determined. But the complexities of trying to determine this distribution should be distinguished from the fundamental method as outlined above. The method itself is quite simple, at least in conception, despite any difficulties that may be involved in attempting to determine the crucial distribution of probabilities of award as a function of the amount of the bid.

We will, then, consider practical ways in which a firm may obtain the necessary information about the distribution of the probabilities of award as a function of the amount of the bid. Since it is customary to announce the bids on contracts after they have been awarded, it is possible to learn the bidding behavior of competitors. We will consider three cases: (1) The competitors for a particular contract are known. (2) The identity of one's competitors is unknown, but the number of competitors is known. (3) Both the identify and the number of competitors are unknown.

First we will consider the case where our competitors in bidding for a particular contract are known. Let us study competitor A. Our information about A consists of every previous contract on which A has bid and for which our firm has made a cost estimate. For every such contract we can determine the ratio of A's bid to our cost estimate (not our "bid"). For example, part of our data on A might look like this:

Contract	Our estimated cost	A's bid	Ratio
1	$8,500	$10,200	1.2
2	22,000	33,000	1.5
3	11,000	15,400	1.4
4	35,000	38,500	1.1
5	9,000	9,000	1.0

The ratio is, of course, simply A's bid divided by our cost estimate. We would continue this procedure for all contracts on which we had the necessary information: our cost estimate and A's bid. We would then summarize all of this information in a table, in which we would give the total number of times that each ratio occurred. This table would look like this:

Ratio of A's bids to our cost estimates	Number of times it occurred
0.9	1
1.0	3
1.1	5
1.2	11
1.3	15
1.4	8
1.5	4
1.6	3
	50

Of course, we would search to discover some influence other than costs (our costs) to account for the difference between our costs and A's bid. It might turn out that A bid lower than our cost estimate when he had not had a contract award for 12 months or more; that he bid much more than our costs when he had recently won a contract that gave him a heavy backlog of work. We have a total of 50 such ratios, and this table gives the frequencies of the various ratios' occurrences. This table contains all of the information available to us for estimating the probability of occurrence of each of the ratios. Consider the ratio 1.2. Out of 50 ratios we find that this ratio occurred 11 times. This indicates that the probability of occurrence of the ratio 1.2 is $11/50 = 0.22$. Similarly, the probability of occurrence of the ratio 1.4 is $8/50 = 0.16$. In short, we can convert the above table into a table of probabilities of occurrence of the various ratios simply by dividing each of the frequencies in the right-hand column by the total number, 50. This gives:

Ratio of A's bid to our cost estimates	Probability of ratio
0.9	0.02
1.0	.06
1.1	.10
1.2	.22
1.3	.30
1.4	.16
1.5	.08
1.6	.06

The sum of the probabilities is 1, as it must be. This table is to be read as follows: With a probability of 0.22, or 22% of the time, competitor A has submitted bids on contracts that were 1.2 times our cost estimate for the contract. We note again that we have used a crude interval in our breakdown of the ratios. This is done solely for the purpose of simplicity in the example. In actual practice one would use a more refined breakdown of the ratios, but the principle would remain exactly the same.

A comparison of this table with that given on page 50 will show that they are completely similar in form. This table is, as that one was, a probability density function. As we pointed out in connection with the table on page 50, to each probability density function corresponds a probability distribution function, and vice versa. Therefore, from our table on competitor A, we can immediately determine the probability distribution function for competitor A. The distribution function will show the probability that a particular bid, expressed as a multiple of our cost estimate, will be lower than the bid of competitor A. Thus, for example, a bid of 0.9 times our cost estimate will be lower than the bid of competitor A with the probability of $1.00 - 0.02 = 0.98$. But this would leave the possibility of tie bids, which is mainly due to the large interval we have used in presenting the ratios. To eliminate this possibility, let us simply lower the bid slightly. Thus, we can say that a bid of 0.89 times our cost estimate will be lower than A's bid with probability of 1.00. A bid of 0.99 times our cost estimate will be lower than A's bid with probability of $1.00 - 0.02 = 0.98$. A bid of 1.09 times our cost estimate will be lower than A's bid with probability of $1.00 - 0.02 - 0.06 = 0.92$. Proceeding similarly, we can obtain the following table:

Bid, as multiple of cost estimate	Probability that bid is lower than bid of A
0.89	1.00
0.99	.98
1.09	.92
1.19	.82
1.29	.60
1.39	.30
1.49	.14
1.59	.06
1.69	.00

This is the required probability distribution function. For any given bid, expressed as a multiple of the cost estimate, it gives the probability that that bid will be lower than the bid of A. Or, if A is our only competitor in bidding for a particular contract, we can say that this table gives the probability of award as a function of the amount of the bid. This statement should sound familiar. If our earlier discussion was correct, this should mean that we already have sufficient information to determine the bid that will give us the maximum expected profit if A is our only competitor.

Let us see whether this is so. Suppose that we are bidding on a contract and that A is our only competitor. As usual, we will let c denote our cost estimate on this contract. Suppose we bid $1.09c$ on this contract. According to our table, the probability will be 0.92 that we will win the contract. If we win the contract we will make a profit of $1.09c - c = 0.09c$. This, of course, is simply the $x - c$ we used above, where $x = 1.09c$. We know that our expected profit is simply the probability of award times $x - c$ -- in this case, then, $0.92(0.09c) = 0.0828c$. If we bid $1.19c$, we have

Expected profit $= 0.82(1.19c - c) = 0.82(.19c) = 0.1558c$.

Proceeding similarly, using the probabilities from the table above, we obtain:

Bid, as multiple of cost estimate	Expected profit where A is only competitor
0.89	$1.00(.89c - c) = -0.11c$
0.99	$.98(.99c - c) = -.0098c$
1.09	$.92(1.09c - c) = .0828c$
1.19	$.82(1.19c - c) = .1558c$
1.29	$.60(1.29c - c) = .1740c$
1.39	$.30(1.39c - c) = .1170c$
1.49	$.14(1.49c - c) = .0786c$
1.59	$.06(1.59c - c) = .0354c$

Clearly, a bid of $1.29c$ gives the maximum expected profit, $0.1740c$. If we use c = $8,000, as in an earlier example, this would give a bid of $10,320 and an expected profit of $1,392. As we expected, then, our empirically obtained information is sufficient to enable us to determine the bid that will maximize our expected profit in the case where A is our only competitor.

What do we do if we have more than one known competitor against us? Let us assume that we are faced with two competitors on a particular contract: A, as above, and B. We could go through precisely the same procedure for obtaining information about B as we did for A. We will not repeat the steps in this procedure because they are in no way different from those illustrated for A above. Granting that we have done this, we would end up with a probability distribution function for B, which would be similar to, but generally different from, that for A. It will then be convenient to present the two probability distribution functions, one for A and one for B, in one table:

Bid, as multiple of cost estimate	Probability that bid is lower than bid of A	B
0.89	1.00	1.00
0.99	.98	.94
1.09	.92	.83
1.19	.82	.65
1.29	.60	.37
1.39	.30	.20
1.49	.14	.10
1.59	.06	.03
1.69	.00	.00

The distribution for A is, of course, the same as that given above. From this table we are able to say immediately that, for example, a bid of 1.09 times cost estimate has a probability of 0.92 of being lower than A's bid, and a probability of 0.83 of being lower than B's bid. Can we deduce from this statement the probability that a bid of 1.09 times the cost estimate will simultaneously be lower than A's bid and B's bid, or, in short, that it will win the award of the contract? Yes, we can do this very simply. The probability of the joint occurrence of two independent events is simply the product of the probabilities of the two events separately. For example, the probability of throwing heads on one coin is simply 1/2. What is the probability of obtaining two heads if two coins are thrown simultaneously? On each coin the probability is 1/2 of obtaining heads; so the probability of getting two heads is 1/2 x 1/2 = 1/4. Similarly, the probability that a bid of 1.09 times the cost estimate will be simultaneously lower than A's bid and B's bid is 0.92 x 0.83 = 0.76. The probability that a bid of 1.19 times the cost estimate will be simultaneously lower than A's bid and B's bid is 0.82 x 0.65 = 0.53. Proceeding in this way, we can obtain for each bid the probability that it is lower than both A's bid and B's bid. To do this, we need only multiply the entries on the same row in the columns under A and B in the table above. This gives:

Bid, as multiple of cost estimate	Probability that bid is simultaneously lower than bids of A and of B
0.89	1.00 x 1.00 = 1.00
0.99	.98 x .94 = .92
1.09	.92 x .83 = .76
1.19	.82 x .65 = .53
1.29	.60 x .37 = .22
1.39	.30 x .20 = .06
1.49	.14 x .10 = .01

But the probability that our bid is simultaneously lower than the bids of A and of B is precisely the probability of award if A and B are our only competitors, as we are assuming. In other words, the table above gives the probability distribution function of award as a function of the amount of the bid. Therefore, once again, we are in possession of the necessary information to enable us to determine the bid with the greatest expected profit. The calculations of the expected profit for each bid proceed exactly as in the various examples we have given earlier. If we bid 1.09 times the cost estimate, the table shows that the probability of award will be 0.76. Our expected profit is, therefore, $0.76(1.09c - c) = 0.0684c$. Our expected profit from a bid of $1.19c$ is $0.53(1.19c - c) = 0.1007c$. Our expected profit from a bid of $1.29c$ is $0.22(1.29c - c) = 0.0638c$. Similarly, the expected profit from each bid can be calculated. The maximum expected profit comes from a bid of $1.19c$ and is $0.1007c$. In terms of our earlier example, where $c = \$8,000$, this means that our bid should be $9,520 with an expected profit of $805.60.

This procedure, granted the necessary data on the past performances of competitors, will work equally well for any number of known competitors. For each competitor we must obtain the probability distribution function showing the probability that a given bid will be lower than the bid of that competitor. Our final probability of award distribution is then determined by multiplying, for each bid, the entries given for each competitor for that bid. This distribution gives the necessary information for calculating the expected profit for each bid, which then enables us to choose the bid with the maximum expected profit. This procedure, therefore, handles the case where the competitors are known.

What can we do when we do not know our competitors? In this event we are no longer able to obtain specific information about the bidding behavior of each competitor as we did above. Our lack of information about the identity of our competitors on a particular contract forces us to utilize less precise information than otherwise. Instead of using information based on specific competitors, we will have to be satisfied with information about our "average" or "typical" competitor. In other words, the best available information in this case is simply the over-all behavior of all our past competitors on those contracts for which we made cost estimates. The procedure to be followed is the same as before, except that we lump all competitors together. We simply combine all the previous ratios of a competitor's bid to our cost estimate into one probability density function. For example, A and B, as above, would be lumped into one probability density function along with all the other competitors for whom we had ratios. From this over-all probability density function of ratios, we can then obtain, as before, the probability distribution function. The final probability distribution function might look like this:

Bid, as multiple of cost estimate	Probability that bid is lower than bid of average competitor
0.89	1.00
0.99	.97
1.09	.90
1.19	.79
1.29	.58
1.39	.35
1.49	.21
1.59	.08
1.69	.02
1.79	.00

This table is equivalent to the table for a single specific competitor, given above. The only difference is that this table is for a single unspecified competitor -- the average competitor. This table should, therefore, be interpreted as follows: the probability is 0.79 that a bid of 1.19 times the cost estimate would be lower than the bid of any single competitor picked at random. Suppose, for example, on a particular contract, that we were faced with only one competitor but that we did not know the identity of this competitor. Then we would use this table to determine the expected profit for each bid. Our calculations would be exactly similar to those we have shown several times above. Notice that the important difference in using this table is that we do not know the identity of our competitor. If we knew that our only competitor was A, then we would use the table for A. Otherwise, <u>we must use the best information we have</u>: the probability distribution function for the average competitor.

Suppose, however, that we do not know the identity of our competitors but that we do know how many of them there are on a particular contract. Can we use the above table to determine the probability of award for each bid? Yes, we can. We simply use this average distribution function as if it applied to each of our unknown competitors and then proceed as in the case of known competitors. This table shows, for example, that a bid of 1.19 times the cost estimate has a probability of 0.79 of being lower than the bid of any one competitor picked at random. Suppose there are two such competitors. The probability that a bid of 1.19 times the cost estimate will be simultaneously lower than the bids of both the competitors is, then, 0.79 x 0.79 = 0.6241. If there are three competitors the probability is 0.79 x 0.79 x 0.79 = 0.4930. If there are four competitors the probability is 0.79 x 0.79 x 0.79 x 0.79 = 0.3895 -- and similarly for each other possible bid. For example, the necessary probability of award distribution function against three unknown competitors is:

Bid, as multiple of cost estimate	Probability that bid is lower than bids of three unknown competitors
0.89	1.00 x 1.00 x 1.00 = 1.00
0.99	.97 x .97 x .97 = .9127
1.09	.90 x .90 x .90 = .7290
1.19	.79 x .79 x .79 = .4930
1.29	.1951
1.39	.0429
1.49	.0093

Of course, the probability that a bid is lower than the bids of three competitors is precisely the probability of award in bidding against the three competitors. Therefore, this table is the required probability of award distribution function as a function of the size of the bid. We can immediately calculate the expected profit for each bid in the usual way. The expected profit for a bid of 1.09c is $0.7290(1.09c - c) = 0.0656c$. The expected profit for a bid of 1.19c is

0.4930(1.19c - c) = 0.0937c. The expected profit for a bid of 1.29c is
0.1951(1.29c - c) = 0.0566c. The maximum expected profit is 0.0937c and is
obtained for a bid of 1.19c. In terms of our earlier example, where c = $8,000,
this would mean that the maximum expected profit is $749.60 and is obtained
by bidding $9,520. It is clear that the same procedure can be followed for
any given number of competitors.

What should we do if we do not know the number of competitors on a
particular contract? The answer to this question is that we must find some
way of obtaining an estimate of the number. Let us consider the effect on our
bid as the number of competitors increases. It is easy to show that, as the
number of competitors increases, the maximum expected profit will be obtained
with smaller bids. We can illustrate this, using the probability distribution
function of the "average" competitor, above. We can calculate the following:

Number of Competitors	Bid with greatest expected profit	Amount of expected profit
1	1.29c	.1682c
2	1.19c	.1386c
3	1.19c	.0937c
4	1.19c	.0750c
5	1.19c	.0585c
6	1.09c	.0478c
7	1.09c	.0430c
8	1.09c	.0387c

It is clear that, as the number of competitors increases, the bid with the maximum expected profit becomes smaller and the amount of expected profit becomes steadily smaller. As the number of competitors gets even larger, the
amount of expected profit goes down steadily toward the breakdown point.
This means simply that the number of competitors is a most important variable
in determining the bid with the maximum expected profit. In the case of an
unknown number of competitors, it is of paramount importance to obtain an
estimate of the number. Once an estimate is available, the above procedure
is followed, using the estimated number of competitors.

We will not discuss any of the various possible methods of estimating the number of competitors. It is similar to other estimation problems and has all the difficulties attendant on most estimation problems. One possibility is to determine whether there has been a relationship between number of bidders and size of contract. If so, it would be possible to use estimated cost as a means of estimating the number of competitors. Perhaps the experience of firm executives will suffice to provide good estimates. Whatever the method of estimation, once the estimate has been obtained, the procedure given above for a known number of competitors is then followed to determine the bid with the maximum expected profit.

PART TWO

BEHAVIORAL SCIENCE FINDINGS

RELEVANT TO PRICING

Like Molière's character who had been speaking prose all his life without realizing it, pricing executives and economists have long been engaged unconsciously in behavioral science studies; for every marketing and pricing executive bases his business decisions upon assumptions about human behavior. There is reason to believe, however, that a more conscious application of these studies can improve our understanding of pricing, pricers, and purchasers' reactions to prices.

The fields of economics, anthropology, sociology, psychology, and political science deal with the perennial problem of how human behavior can be explained and predicted; and each of these fields is concerned with a different facet of individual and social behavior. The last decade has seen the growing convergence of three of these fields -- psychology, sociology, and anthropology. Increasingly, they are adopting the same terminology and appear to be developing a common core of concepts and data. There is, furthermore, a growing movement toward bringing together all of the social sciences concerned with group behavior. [1]

Many other fields have already profited from the application of a behavioral science approach. Among the broad fields that have been enriched by this approach are mental health and illness, community leadership, urban and suburban living, adult education, economic development of underdeveloped areas, tolerance education, and industrial relations. Within a large area of

---

[1] The attempts to unify these fields can be seen in publications like Human Relations, a joint British-United States journal devoted to group processes and published since 1946; and Behavioral Science, an American journal working toward a unified theory of behavior. Interdisciplinary publications like the 1956 book Toward a General Theory of Action (the report of one university seminar on integrating several approaches to behavior) also represent significant attempts by outstanding specialists to blend their knowledge for the greater good of common knowledge.

marketing, much attention has recently been paid, with considerable success, to the applications of behavioral science in advertising.

Economists themselves have for many decades drawn upon the other social sciences. A major contribution to economic theory was the demonstration by Lord Keynes that interest rates do not influence saving very much, but that saving may be strongly affected by nonpecuniary considerations. Thorstein Veblen's famous thesis -- that rarity, rather than beauty or utility, is the chief criterion of the purchases of the leisure class -- represents an early application of the use of psychology and anthropology to the study of prices.

Economists and students of marketing have for years prepared analyses of "the behavior of prices," and have abstracted various principles of price movement. The behavioral scientist would be inclined to question whether price-setters or customers behave in a manner that lends itself to easy generalization; and he would stress the need to study the behavior of buyers and sellers, and the interactions among pricers and purchasers, in order to establish their patterns of behavior. A realistic analysis of the pricing process requires understanding of the nonrational elements included in a pricing decision. It also should explain what kind of person would do what under which circumstances -- thus recognizing the interrelated roles of personality, culture, and the social system in any price decision. The personality of the pricer, the culture of which he is a part, and the larger system within which the pricer and his purchaser function -- all of these must be considered in order to clarify as many as possible of the dimensions of pricing behavior.

The behavioral science approach would emphasize that there is an interaction process, as a result of which an individual price-setter, functioning within a group setting, establishes a given price. Consumers of the product perceive price among many other dimensions of the product; the price is one of several elements in the purchaser's decision to purchase or not to purchase, or to repurchase the product.

Businessmen differ in the extent to which they feel they can influence their environment, and this is reflected in their price decisions. Information about the pricer's expectations is important for any discussion of pricing. How the pricer feels that the future will affect him is reflected in everything he does. Another dimension of pricer behavior is his role. Every pricer has a multiple role: he is not only a businessman but also, since he himself purchases many items, a consumer of priced objects. This multiplicity of roles is likely to be reflected in price decisions.

Thus, we have good reason to expect that the various social sciences, individually and as a group, have been developing valuable material and insights, which may provide understanding of many previously unrecognized facets of price and pricing. In the following chapters, certain behavioral science concepts and findings regarding perception, attitudes, and group processes are presented; and the ways in which these findings can enhance our knowledge of pricing are discussed. Because of the enormous amount of behavioral science research in these three areas, only a minimal summary of the relevant literature is presented. This material is relevant to a number of areas within marketing; however, only some pricing implications are discussed -- and even these implications are meant to be suggestive rather than definitive.

The following sections deal with only three of many recognized spheres of behavioral science. These three spheres are not all-inclusive by any means; as they are construed here, however, they embrace most the entire corpus of behavioral science. No area of behavioral science where one could reasonably expect to get much insight into pricing has been omitted.

In reading these materials, the reader should remember that they have been prepared not for behavioral scientists but for marketing specialists. Moreover, they do not claim to provide an exhaustive catalogue of applications to marketing.

The main objective of this material is to show the value of behavioral science findings for operating executives and for teachers of marketing. It is to be viewed also as a test of a new technique for making technical and complex materials of one branch of science available to practitioners in another field.

CHAPTER IV

PERCEPTION AND PRICING

Human behavior necessarily reflects what people believe their situation to be rather than the actual situation itself. As is explained in the following section, substantial differences often exist between what actually is and what most people perceive. Misperception, to some degree, is the common rather than the exceptional or abnormal practice.

Marketing executives will admit that they constantly try to make their product and their total "offer" look better than it really is. They take measures to make their products appear more durable, modern, carefully finished, moderate in price, desired by most customers, etc., than is actually the case. In short, they strive to create misperceptions that are in their own self-interest. Therefore, it is of genuine vocational value to such persons to learn how to put the best face on their offerings and to understand how prospective customers will view them.

The field of pricing, no less than most other aspects of marketing, presents opportunities to influence customer perception. Psychological pricing, for example, is a virtual marketing specialty devoted to finding prices that seem lower than they really are. "Sales" are almost always accompanied by a change in physical appearance of the seller's premises to create the feeling in customers that they are attending a carnival at which prizes are given away. Under such circumstances, customers apparently see different things when they look at the same price tag than they would perceive without the carnival atmosphere.

These two, of many possible, examples suggest that it might prove valuable to persons responsible for pricing to study the views of the various schools of psychology regarding the perception process. These views are presented briefly in the first section of this chapter. The second section then relates them directly to the subject of pricing.

BEHAVIORAL SCIENCE FINDINGS ON PERCEPTION

Philosophers have made heroic efforts to establish what is meant by "reality." The famous British philosopher Bishop Berkeley even suggested that "reality" does not exist at all unless it is perceived by someone. Modern psychologists have become deeply interested in studying the individual's perception of "reality." Their interests extend far beyond studies of the sense organs; for perception, as it is currently defined, is more than sensation. It is the dynamic process by which we register what is in the environment -- the process by which the perceiver or beholder gives meaning to the raw material provided by the external world. This definition, it will be shown, recognizes -- among other things -- the perceiver's own feelings, values, needs, aspirations, and fears. It is completely normal to perceive in a personalized way; indeed, perception essentially represents personalized misperception.

Writing several decades ago, psychiatrist Alfred Adler effectively explained why everybody perceives things differently: ". . . a perception is never to be compared with a photographic image because something of the peculiar and individual quality of the person who perceives is inextricably bound up with it. One does not perceive everything that one sees. No two human beings react in quite the same way to the identical picture; if we ask them what they have perceived they will give very diverse answers. Everyone is capable of reconfiguring and rearranging his contacts with the outer world to fit his life pattern. The individuality and uniqueness of a human being consists in what he perceives and how he perceives it . . . ."[1]

The human perceptual mechanism has many facets. It enables the individual to add meaning to what his senses register; and it may prevent him from seeing things that are quite obvious, or from understanding the significance of what he does see.

Human beings also have a faculty of subception, a process by which perception takes place even though there is an absolute minimum of cues or stimuli. One form of subception dramatically indicates the strange and powerful nature of the perceptual process: that is, it has been established that persons may literally not see or hear perfectly obvious things because they are able to "sense" that these things will be extremely painful to perceive. Apparently, their perceptual mechanism unconsciously anticipates something threatening and either does not admit the stimuli to consciousness or distorts them so that they can be accepted by the perceiver without insupportable pain.

The very process of sense perception suggests the unusual nature and power of the perceptual mechanism. In human vision, for example, all visual

----

[1]Alfred Adler, Understanding Human Nature (New York: Greenberg, 1929), pp. 47-48.

functions require cortical connections. The brain processes all visual phenomena into the perceptions we receive. Each eye gets a somewhat different picture of the same object or situation; the brain amalgamates and adjusts the two images into one. The image on the eye's retina is upside down and inverted from right to left; the brain enables us to see right side up. The brain takes unclear stimuli and makes them clear. The brain screens phenomena: without its work, our senses would deliver a jumble of meaningless sensations to our consciousness -- like hundreds of television programs telecast simultaneously over the same channel. With the intervention of the brain, we receive only one program and it is coherent; however, to some degree -- in the process of producing this coherent program out of the hundreds of programs in the air -- the brain is likely to censor and edit, to suit its own fancy, parts of the program that we do receive.

To understand why differences in perception occur, it is important to face the implications of one fact: a person cannot perceive and take account of everything to which his senses are exposed. Any person whose eyes are open has before him, at any given moment, enormously more stimuli than his eyes can focus upon. Likewise, the ears and skin are able to record only a small fraction of the sensations that are available to them. As a result, the sense organs must perceive selectively. The process of selection of a few from among many stimuli varies from individual to individual. We all know that Mr. Smith differs from Mr. Jones, but only recently have psychologists documented that they differ substantially in the way they perceive reality. They have been examining, for example, why Jones will describe a glass as half full of water, whereas Smith will describe the same glass as half empty.

Clearly, humans can respond to something only if they perceive it. To understand human behavior, therefore, an understanding of the perceptual process is required. Most perception is explicable by the views of one or another of the several schools of psychology. These schools try to explain how we perceive reality and why each person's perception of the world around him probably differs from anyone else's perception of it. The differences, of course, are very great if one considers the severe distortions of perception found in some psychiatric patients; but mild distortions occur in normal persons as well.

There are three major schools of perception; the psychoanalytic school, which emphasizes mechanisms like "cathexis" and "projection"; the Gestalt school, which utilizes concepts like "wholes" and "figure-ground relationships"; and the social-perception school, which concentrates on the "needs" of the perceiver. All of these schools of psychology emphasize that perception is idiosyncratic and highly personalized. In appraising the three major schools, one should compare the sources of data on which each one builds. Psychoanalytic data derive from the treatment of many patients, whose mechanisms for perceptual distortion become visible to the psychoanalyst.

The Gestalt and social-perception data generally are derived from controlled experiments.

Psychoanalytic Views of Perception

The psychoanalytic school, composed of outstanding contributors like Freud, Jones, and Abraham,[2] began around 1910. Its members, who are in general completely committed to the psychoanalytic point of view, explain perception mainly by considering variations in the extent to which individuals invest objects with emotional energy.[3] The emotional energy that attaches to an object reflects the individual's previous experiences and associations (usually in early childhood) with related objects, even though he may not be able to recall the experiences. Cathexis is the name given to the process by which an object achieves emotional meaning for an individual. Objects that are highly cathected stand out and are observed much more readily by the perceiver than are other objects; those that are not invested with emotional energy are less likely to be perceived -- although, when perceived at all, they are usually less likely to be misperceived.

Misperception is likely to occur directly to the degree to which an object is cathected, for the perceiver's past associations and experiences ordinarily will be injected into his current observations. Thus, as a result of cathexis, he may prefer madeleine cookies to petits fours -- simply because the madeleines are associated with an early experience that has great meaning for him, whereas petits fours have no such association. In Marcel Proust's great novel Remembrance of Things Past, the hero is reminded of important experiences in his early life by tasting madeleine cookies dipped into tea; because he had cathected the cookies so strongly, he is now transported in imagination back to the past.

Another mechanism that psychoanalysts employ to explain perception is projection -- a process by which individuals transfer their inner drives, or needs, fears, fantasies, and desires   onto external objects, even when those objects are neutral with respect to needs or drives. Thus, a neutral inkblot may look like a steak dinner to a hungry man. It is widely accepted that projection of our needs and fears can color our perception of everyday reality. Freud's findings in this area -- namely, that individuals may perceive numbers, clothing, furniture, and other persons in terms of previous emotional meanings -- opened up an entire field for subsequent investigation.[4] Psychoanalysts

---

[2]Sigmund Freud, The Psychopathology of Everyday Life (London: Ernest Benn, 1913; Ernest Jones, Free Associations (New York: Basic Books, 1959); Karl Abraham, Selected Papers (London: Hogarth, 1934).

[3]Ruth L. Munroe, Schools of Psychoanalytic Thought (New York: Dryden, 1955), pp. 97-104.

[4]Freud, op. cit.

have documented many cases in which the emotional predisposition of normal people has led them to attach special emotional meanings to all manner of objects, situations, or people. They have established that this process is normal and pervasive. As already explained, when special emotional meaning attaches to objects, the manner in which they are perceived is affected; under such circumstances, the observer ordinarily adds something to reality to create a misperception. The psychoanalytic mechanism of <u>identification</u> involves our establishing a sense of identity by cathecting specific people in our environment.

The psychoanalytic views regarding the role of cathexis, projection, and identification in perception have been absorbed by the general field of psychology. Rather than offering alternative explanations for perception, the other schools of psychology suggest additional elements that the psychoanalytic school possibly overlooks.

Gestalt Views of Perception

The Gestalt school, which began around 1920, includes distinguished contributors like Köhler, Koffka, and Wertheimer.[5] <u>Gestalt</u> is a German word that can be roughly translated as "whole." Gestalt psychology emphasizes that we see things as wholes rather than as a collection of discrete parts.[6] It stresses that we superimpose our own preconceived total view of reality -- the Gestalt -- on what we see.

If, for example, we see a figure, like ∪, we are more likely to describe it as an incomplete circle or a poorly made letter C than as a curved line, because of our long experience in seeing things as wholes.

A corollary of the Gestalt approach is that we perceive an object in relation to other objects with which we compare it -- even as we define objects in this manner. We make comparisons in terms of <u>anchorage points of perception</u>, which form part of the context within which we perceive. These anchorage points vary widely among individuals.

Gestalt psychologists maintain that the <u>context</u> in which something is perceived gives it meaning to the beholder. An outstanding example of the importance of context could be seen at the time of the panic resulting from the Orson Welles radio broadcast of an "Invasion from Mars."[7] Since this broad-

[5]Wolfgang Köhler, <u>Gestalt Psychology</u>, 2nd ed. (New York: Liveright, 1947); Kurt Koffka, <u>Principles of Gestalt Psychology</u> (New York: Liveright, 1937); Max Wertheimer, <u>Productive Thinking</u> (New York: Harper & Brothers, 1945).

[6]Koffka, <u>op. cit.</u>

[7]Hadley Cantril, <u>The Invasion from Mars</u> (Princeton: Princeton University Press, 1940).

cast took the form of a "regular" news broadcast, and occurred during a period of international tension just after the Munich pact, the audience's context of belief and expectations made it relatively easy to perceive the broadcast as reality, so that thousands of people actually left their homes to seek help.

Another dimension of Gestalt perception theory is the distinction between figure and ground. We most easily perceive the figure, which may be defined as the central and most directly visible component of a visual stimulus, because it has a relatively more cohesive pattern or shape; the ground, which may be defined as the background of the stimulus field, is more difficult to perceive. Not all parts of a stimulus field, however, have the same prominence and meaning for different persons. Studies of rumors, in which attempts are made to trace how the rumor has spread from one person to another, demonstrate that people perceive some components of the rumor as figure and others as ground; they tend to perceive (and to pass on) the material that constitutes the figure -- for them -- and not the material that constitutes the ground.[8] Rumor studies have also demonstrated that a number of other perceptual factors are operative in the transmission of a rumor: closure (the need for a meaningful whole), bizarreness (retention of unusual words), movement (unusually high retention of comments involving action), etc.

Gestalt psychologists have developed the concept of silent organization to explain the influence upon perception of factors outside the perceiver's awareness. This concept accounts for the formation of frames of reference. The silent organization creates a framework or standpoint from which we typically look at things; we use these frames of reference to help us perceive external objects of all kinds. The neural structure of the brain, according to this view, is prepared to perceive in certain ways. If we see an inch of metal bobbing up and down and moving forward on the other side of a fence in the rain, we are likely to perceive far more than this fragmentary piece of evidence; most people will probably perceive a man or woman walking under an umbrella in the rain. This example illustrates the Gestalt principle of closure, the tendency or need to complete an observed figure in order to give it meaning.

A related Gestalt principle is that of outstandingness -- certain special qualities that some objects may have, which makes one's perception of them easier and/or more lasting than would be the case merely on the basis of their physical qualities alone. Thus, the last car in a seventy-car freight train is likely to have more outstandingness than the thirty-second car.

An offshoot of Gestalt principles is the concept of primacy and recency in perception, which explains that the sequence of events and phenomena

---

[8] Gordon W. Allport and Leo J. Postman, "The Basic Psychology of Rumor," Transactions of the New York Academy of Sciences, 8 (1945), 61-81.

affects our perceptions of them. Recency explains why recent experiences tend to be more vivid than early ones; primacy, why first acts in a series tend to be favored. In one experiment, Asch read two lists of traits that were allegedly possessed by two different groups of people.[9] The traits were actually the same, but they were presented in different sequences in the two lists. Those participating in the test gave markedly different descriptions of the persons in the two groups; therefore, Asch was led to the conclusion that the first few traits attributed to each group provided a frame of reference against which the subsequent characteristics were perceived. Thus, the order in which we perceive things establishes a frame of reference and affects what they mean to us.

How perceptions of personality and situations are determined by a total configuration was dramatically demonstrated in a related experiment by Asch.[10] He gave students two lists of qualities attributed to two hypothetical persons and asked the subjects to describe these persons. The first list contained the words intelligent, skillful, industrious, warm, determined, practical, cautious. The second list was similar to the first except that the word cold replaced warm. The description of the two persons varied substantially: a change in only the one quality produced a central change in the entire perception of the person.

The importance of another perceptual factor, set -- which denotes a particular expectation to perceive -- was illustrated in another experiment.[11] The subjects were shown playing cards, some of which had color and suit reversed. Because the subjects had a set for the expected color-suit combinations, they took longer to recognize an incongruous card than to recognize the standard cards. After some practice, they could recognize the reversed cards more readily. This experiment illustrates the strength of a person's established perceptual schema, when it is applied to a new perception situation. It also shows that we can quickly adjust to new situations involving perception; the subjects eventually developed a new set for the unused cards.

Gestalt theory emphasizes that each culture has its own sets or expectations of perception. Thus, in the Müller-Lyer illusion illustrated below, most people in our culture would see B as longer than A, although the two lines are the same length. The Torres Strait islanders, on the other hand, are

---

[9] Solomon E. Asch, "Forming Impressions of Personality," Journal of Abnormal and Social Psychology, 41 (1946), 258-290.

[10] Solomon E. Asch, Social Psychology (Englewood Cliffs, N.J.: Prentice-Hall, 1952), pp. 207-217.

[11] Jerome S. Bruner and Leo J. Postman, "On the Perception of Incongruity: A Paradigm," Journal of Personality, 18 (1949), 206-212.

less susceptible to this distorted perception than we are -- possibly because they so often work with spears in fishing expeditions.

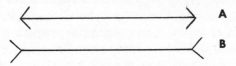

Such experiments have demonstrated that cultural conditioning affects the frames of reference that are widely held in a society, and therefore affects the nature of perception. Gestalt principles focus on the qualities of a stimulus as well as on the perceiver. Gestalt emphasis thus differs radically from psychoanalytic approaches, which focus almost entirely on the perceiver's emotional expectations.

Social Perception

The third important school of perceptual psychology can loosely be called the social-perception school. The social-perception school emerged as a central force around 1945, and is a less tightly knit and formally defined group than the other two. It is composed of a number of distinguished psychologists whose views do not resemble one another as much as do those of Gestalt and psychoanalytic theorists. Therefore -- although many books have summarized the main tenets of the psychoanalytic and Gestalt points of view -- it is relatively difficult to summarize the views of the social-perception school. There has been no book as yet devoted to this school; its findings are contained in a large number of journal articles and monographs.

It is nevertheless safe to say that American psychology has moved in the the direction of the social-perception approach. This approach has been called the "new look," both because it represents a genuinely new emphasis and because it became popular at the time of the "new look" in women's fashions introduced by designer Christian Dior after World War II. This approach stresses mainly the social and need determinants of perception. It explains that the unique conscious or unconscious preconceptions of each perceiver affect what he sees "out there." Emphasizing that the environment is relatively meaningless and inchoate until it is given shape and form by the beholder, this approach makes the unique and special qualities of the perceiver the central element in perceptual theory.

Social-perception experiments have demonstrated that we are likely to perceive things on the basis of what we want or expect them to be, as a result of our previous learning and training as well as our past and current motivations and needs. Since many of our wants and expectations are related to social factors, our perceptions are to a considerable degree socially determined. The social-perception school emphasizes childhood motivations far less than do the psychoanalysts, and it emphasizes the structural aspects of perceptual stimuli less than does the Gestalt school.

The social-perception viewpoint suggests that people can perceive only those elements of the environment that they are "ready" to perceive. The organism is prepared (eingestellt) for a relatively limited range of elements of reality and events at any one time. So "tuned in," the organism selects certain stimuli from what is "out there," just as a television set can get only one station at a time. The individual's greatest need, according to this view, is to perceive that which confirms his previous patterns of behavior. When stimuli (reality) continue to confirm a person's behavior patterns, he is likely to achieve a stable perceptual organization. If confirmation is not obtained -- because there are, after all, limits to an individual's perceptual distortion -- the normal individual's expectations shift until his needs can be confirmed by what is "out there." Thus, stable perceptual equilibrium is restored.

Studies by anthropologists dramatically illustrate this proposition. They have found that some Pacific tribes cannot separate green from blue wool. The individual's eyes undoubtedly have the capacity to distinguish between the wave lengths of the two colors, but they cannot "see" blue because their language has no word for blue; it simply is not "there." [12] Other studies have shown that the Chuckchee have enormous difficulty in matching different-colored yarns with the standard colored yarns used in the Holmgren test, because their vocabulary does not have words for many of the colors; however, they have words for and can differentiate two dozen shades of reindeer pelt. We perceive, in other words, only what we are ready for. If we are especially ready to perceive something, we do so very easily.

Two social psychologists have provided an interesting example of the way in which needs influence perception. [13] They found that if two men were sitting at a lunchroom and one was hungry while the other was thirsty, each one would notice a different part of the luncheon menu. One man would see drinks and some "other" things. The other man would see food and "other" things. A pioneer study in social perception similarly found that the need for food in adults and children has a significant effect both on their associations to words and on what they see in drawings. [14] For example, some hungry subjects perceived a baby with his finger pointing as "sticking his finger in the pie," while some non-hungry subjects saw the baby "pointing to a toy."

---

[12] W. A. Kepner, "Observations on Color Perception among the Visayans of Leyte Island," Science, 22 (1905), 680-683.

[13] David Krech and Richard S. Crutchfield, Theory and Problems of Social Psychology (New York: McGraw-Hill, 1948), p. 88.

[14] R. Nevitt Sanford, "The Effects of Abstinence from Food upon Imaginal Processes," Journal of Psychology, 2 (1936), 129-136; 3 (1937), 145-159.

Another noted study found that labor and management representatives perceived a strike quite differently.[15]

Data on the influence of needs on perception are also derived from experiments that make use of special experimental equipment to create visual distortions. For instance, a series of major experiments conducted by Adelbert Ames, Jr., at Dartmouth and Princeton, employed distorted rooms and special lenses for this purpose. In one of these experiments, the Honi phenomenon -- a dramatic shift in frames of reference -- was shown to exist.[16] In an Ames distorted room, the subject usually saw the room itself as normal, although a face shown in a window appeared to change in size depending on the window in which it was perceived. When the subject, however, saw the face of his or her spouse in a window, the subject generally perceived the room, rather than the face of the spouse, as distorted. This Honi phenomenon was found in almost all of 32 subjects, even though 24 of the 32 subjects had been married for less than a year. It could be concluded that the subject had a strong need to think of his mate as "normal" and undistorted, but had no such need with regard to the room. Other Ames experiments have demonstrated other cultural components in perception.

Social-perception research has demonstrated that our economic circumstances may have a kind of "ruboff" on our perception in ways of which we may be unaware. In a famous experiment, ten-year-old children of normal intelligence were divided into two matched groups, one from prosperous parents and the other from a slum area.[17] They were asked to attempt to match the size of coins of various denominations with a circle of light cast on a screen. The subjects could control the diameter of the circle on the screen. In another test, they were asked to describe the size of various coins ranging from a penny to a half dollar in value. In both tests, the group of slum children overestimated the size of the coins much more often than did the children from prosperous families, with the overestimation in direct relation to the values of the coins; the larger the money value of the coin, the more likely they were to overestimate its size. When holding the coin in the palm of their hand, in another phase of the same experiment, the poor children again were significantly more likely to overestimate the size of the coin than were the rich children.

---

[15]George W. Hartmann and Theodore N. Newcomb, eds. Industrial Conflict (New York: Cordon, 1939), pp. 179-182.

[16]W. J. Wittreich, "The Honi Phenomenon: A Case of Selective Perceptual Distortion," Journal of Abnormal and Social Psychology, 47 (1952), 705-712.

[17]Jerome S. Bruner and Cecile C. Goodman, "Value and Need as Organizing Factors in Perception," Journal of Abnormal and Social Psychology, 42 (1947), 33-44.

The experiment suggests that the possession or lack of money influences our ability to perceive even the specific kind of reality represented by the size of a coin.

The school of social perception has thus systematically explored a variety of social and personal factors that distort the perceiver's impressions of the world.

An Eclectic View

Each of the schools of perception can adduce data to substantiate its own major tenets. Modern psychology is attempting to synthesize these schools and emerge with an eclectic viewpoint, which draws on them as needed to explain a given phenomenon. Most psychologists believe that no one of these schools by itself is adequate, but that, taken together, they can explain almost all perceptual phenomena.

The eclectic view of perceptual psychology attaches central significance to the perceiver's mood, temperament, and mental set. Mood provides an additional dimension, which, although relatively brief and short-lived, exerts an important effect on perception. In one experiment, subjects were hypnotized and placed into happy, critical, or anxious moods, in order to determine whether their perception would be affected by their moods.[18] While under hypnosis, subjects in each of the three moods were shown the same set of pictures and asked to describe what they had seen. The different moods had a clearly visible and measurable effect on what they perceived as well as on the meaning they attached to what they perceived. Subjects who had been made critical reported more querulous content, those who had been made anxious perceived more anxiety content, and those who were hypnotized into a happy mood saw happier content.

Temperament, a more permanent element of personality than mood, reflects such deep-rooted qualities as basal metabolism, body build, and degree of languor or rapidity in the pace of living. Sheldon has documented the considerable extent to which temperament influences perception.[19]

As noted above, in the discussion of the playing-card experiment, a mental set that influences perception may be relatively short-lived. If someone is considering the purchase of an overcoat, he is likely to be very alert to the details of his friends' overcoats because his mental set is toward overcoats.

---

[18] Clarence Leuba and C. Lucas, "The Effects of Attitudes on Description of Pictures," Journal of Experimental Psychology, 35 (1945), 517-524.

[19] William H. Sheldon and S. S. Stevens, The Varieties of Temperament (New York: Harper & Brothers, 1942).

At other times, however, he will probably ignore such details. Our social role also helps determine our mental set. Thus, the lawyer, the policeman, and the thief simultaneously walking along the same block in a large city will each perceive different stimuli.

APPLICATION OF BEHAVIORAL SCIENCE MATERIALS ON PERCEPTION TO PRICING

How can persons concerned with establishing price or understanding how others do so make use of the foregoing discussion of the perception process? To what extent does it explain phenomena that have been unfathomable heretofore? Does it suggest questions or errors that have passed unrecognized up to now? In an effort to answer these questions, we shall examine three problems: (1) Will an understanding of the perceptual biases of price-setters (if, as we suspect, such biases exist) lead to interesting discoveries about the pricing process? (2) Are there widespread perceptual biases among consumers that persons setting price would find it helpful to know? (3) Are there important situations in which sellers' and consumers' misperceptions are incompatible and cause special difficulties?

Perceptual Biases of Price-Setters

An examination of the many factors that are considered by the average executive who is making a decision about price might uncover several typical misperceptions of considerable significance.

The price-setter will invariably be concerned with such factors as the following: his own costs; the prices charged by competitors; the merits of the products that his firm sells relative to the offerings of rivals; the responses of firms that resell the product to any price decision he might reach; the possible reactions of suppliers, labor, and government to various prices he might charge; and, perhaps above all, the responses of prospective customers. In taking these factors into account, the price-setter will rely upon his own perception of and explanation for the existing situation. When he is provided with extensive market-research information, his perceptions may not depart significantly from reality; in the more usual case, where he is compelled to rely primarily on his personal impressions and observations, and on the views expressed by his colleagues, the opportunity for misperception skyrockets.

It is possible to examine each of the factors considered by price-setters and to speculate about the misperceptions that probably exist -- if any. If such an undertaking were based upon a careful study of price-setters, it would have particular value. For example, a tendency for sellers to misperceive (or miscalculate) their costs has been charged by most economists who have been concerned with the field of pricing, and underlies their criticism of average-cost or cost-plus pricing.

In this section, only one important perceptual bias of price-setters will be considered: the tendency for price-setters to misperceive the importance of price to their customers. It is suggested that because most price-setters exaggerate the sensitivity of the customer to modest changes in price, they may systematically charge less than the price that would provide maximum advantage to their firm.

To understand this misperception, one must recognize the unrepresentative character of the customers to whom executives talk or about whom they hear from their colleagues. In almost every line of business, it seems that most customers are docile and rarely heard from; a very small number, on the other hand, are quick to register complaints -- at length and with considerable vehemence. Even if the price-setter consciously recognizes that the complainers are a special group, he will usually attach more importance to their statements than their numbers warrant. Consequently, since the outspoken customers are also the most critical, the price-setter probably perceives his customers as being discerning about product features and quality, etc., and quick to notice prices that are not exactly in line with those charged by some rivals. In other words, he may perceive the large majority, who are actually docile and loyal and possibly unobserving, as having attributes that only a tiny minority possess. As a result, he could reach mistaken conclusions about price.

Thus, the typical price-setter probably believes that most of his customers will know about rival company offerings that are more attractive than those of his firm. He may not perceive that many of his customers will consider the products offered by these companies as lower in quality than those of his firm; that many of his customers will consider his firm's price low because some other companies are charging more than his firm; and that many customers will simply assume that other firms charge more, even when they do not. To the extent that the average price-setter misperceives in this manner, he will feel impelled to match the very lowest prices in the industry; he will thereby fail to capitalize on whatever loyalty he may possess among customers and on his customers' misperceptions of the prices charged by his firm and other firms.

The misperceptions of price-setters that stem from the unrepresentative information they obtain are more obvious than other misperceptions -- which, however, have the same effect. The very fact that the price-setter derives his income from and spends most of his time thinking about price is likely to distort his perceptions so that he exaggerates the importance of price to his customers. Similarly, he is likely to be relatively emotional and calculating about his own purchases -- especially his purchases of the items that his firm produces. As a result, he may frequently attribute to others the same degree of concern with price and the same ability to assess quality differences that he himself has.

To the extent that this misperception is widespread and strong, it could be highly significant. From a broad social viewpoint, it may contribute to a desirable intensity of price competition. From the standpoint of the individual businessman, it represents a failing in employees, against which business owners must guard if they would obtain maximum profits. It is a circumstance that could easily pass unnoticed if one were not alerted by the findings of social science to look for significant and stable misperceptions of reality.

Perceptual Biases of Consumers

It appears to be well established that the "sound" of a price affects the sales of some products to a considerable degree. There are apparently many qualities of a price that make it "sound right." The notion that prices have a "sound" suggests that some prices seem different than they really are and therefore promote misperceptions of the real price. Many price-setters are convinced that some prices are "psychologically right," and the quest for such prices has become something of a specialty.

There are some interesting cases where consumers have objected to a price because it "sounded" too low. For instance, when electric clocks were first introduced, consumers were slow to buy them because they were priced relatively low compared to quality spring-wind clocks. Consumers apparently felt that a quality clock could not be sold so cheaply. The clocks were withdrawn from the market and reintroduced subsequently at a higher price that "sounded" better -- after which they sold more successfully. Similarly, on another occasion, hosiery worth $2.00 was placed on sale for $1.00 in a particular department store. It drew a minimal response. The same stockings were later offered at $1.19 and drew a large response. Investigation helped to explain the paradox (of which there are many examples): The $1.19 sales price actually suggested a better value, and was perceived as such by consumers, than the $1.00 price. When offered at $1.00, the stockings were regarded by most consumers as relatively low and unacceptable in quality, and were not even perceived to be reduced in price. At $1.19, on the other hand, many customers perceived that the hosiery had been reduced from a much higher price.

The total context against which a product and price are perceived has a great effect on consumer behavior. For example, plastic parts on a camera are likely to be perceived as a sign of low quality, while plastic on automobile seat covers is usually associated with covers of high quality. The same softness of fabric that would be taken as evidence of high quality in a man's expensive suit (i.e., a high content of cashmere wool) would be perceived as proof of low quality if the suit were sold at a low price; consumers would attribute the soft feel to the low proportion of worsted fibers. An object sold in a bargain basement will be perceived by most customers to be quite different from the same object sold in an expensive store -- illustrating the Gestalt emphasis on the background against which we see objects.

Another Gestalt phenomenon, the concept of anchorage points of perception, may help to explain the consumer's comparison of a brand's price with that of competing brands. Consumers of any brand are not likely to know the prices of most -- or even many -- competing brands. (There may be important exceptions, such as possibly the price of automobiles; even here, however, consumers would know list prices rather than the prices actually quoted by dealers.) The purchaser of one brand of toothbrush is not likely to know the prices of the other major toothbrush brands, especially if they are not sold in the same store -- as is often the case. Lacking such knowledge, the consumer is able to perceive the price of the brand he purchased in the desired relationship to other brands he might have bought. Since most consumers want to believe that they are not paying more for the same product than the next person, they will perceive the prices of brands they did not purchase to be equal to or higher than the prices they paid. They will often accumulate these perceptions as they pass counters in shops that they enter for other purposes, in windows, in advertisements, etc.; for they need reassurances that they have not been overcharged, and they want to be prepared to justify their purchases if challenged. The particular prices they will remember and will perceive typically will be those that justify their purchase.

The marketer generally is able to influence the context within which the customer perceives his product. By advertising and public relations, by his choice of channels of distribution, his display arrangements, the manner in which price is marked on the product, and by the different items that he includes in his line, the marketer may influence potential customers' perceptions of his brand's relative price. The very print in which a price is expressed lead many customers to perceive it in a particular way.

Another type of misperception that may be advantageous to the marketer is the multiple-unit price. To take an example, consider the price of three units for 79 cents. The consumer, especially if he is not accustomed to seeing the item sold in multiple units, may respond positively to the multiple-item offer; because it bears a "confused" price, he may assume that the particular price offers a large-quantity discount. The consumer who wishes to or has a need to perceive his purchase as a bargain can easily do so because of the unclear unit cost.

Up to this point, common consumer misperceptions have been discussed. In recent years, a new concept introduced into marketing discussions has helped to account for buyer perceptions and misperceptions. This concept -- of the brand image -- is one of the most widely discussed marketing subjects of the present time. As a result of widespread discussion of the brand image concept, most marketing specialists conclude that a favorable brand image is one of the most valuable assets that a firm can possess and that most firms, whether or not they tried to create it, have a fairly distinct image among their customers.

Studies of the image of different makes of automobiles in the mid-1950s first brought the image approach into national prominence.[20] These studies showed that people have very different perceptions of different makes of automobiles, and that these different perceptions seem to have little relation to the realistic differences among the automobiles. Many people had vaguely realized that there were differences in the connotations of individual automobile brands; formalization of the concept of brand image helped to clarify thinking on the subject. Once the differences in consumers' images of different brands of automobiles were set forth, the concept of the brand image was accepted enthusiastically by most marketing specialists.

Proponents of the so-called image approach suggest that the consumer often does not perceive the intrinsic qualities of a product realistically, but through a screen of meanings associated with the product. Thus, he will probably perceive an automobile in terms of prestige, luxury, social situation, and status symbols -- rather than in terms of economy of operation, durability, trade-in value, etc.

An image is a complex of impressions, anecdotes, experiences, advertising, and other communications. The qualities of a particular brand image are sometimes difficult to describe, but the existence of this image, and its importance in specific cases, can scarcely be denied. Most persons who are interested in clothes, for example, have a clear and quite similar picture of stores like Brooks Brothers and Saks Fifth Avenue. Such an image surely affects the way they perceive the quality of apparel and the prices in each store, because they enter the store with certain preconceptions of what they will find. The psychoanalytic principle of identification (with regular shoppers of these stores) and the Gestalt principle of outstandingness help to explain the image of these stores, and the social-perception school would emphasize the individual shopper's status needs in establishing his perception of the store.

What are the main components, in addition to price, that enter into a brand image? There are at least four such components for most products.[21] First, the consumer's impression of the firm that makes the product. Thus, the general reputation of General Motors and of Procter and Gamble ordinarily affects consumers' perceptions of the products made by these companies, when their subordinate companies call attention to the large corporation of which they are a part.

---

[20]Automobiles, What They Mean to Americans (Chicago: The Chicago Tribune, 1954).

[21]Charles Winick, "How To Find Out What Kind of Image You Have," in Developing the Corporate Image, Lee H. Bristol, Jr., ed. (New York: Scribner's, 1960), pp. 23-40.

Second, the consumer's opinions of the kinds of people who ordinarily use the brand: that is, is the brand bought mainly by old spinsters, elegant bachelors, active young women, housewives of large urban families, or the like? Belief that the brand is purchased by some particular group of persons gives it intangible but often strong and important qualities in the perceptions of most consumers.

Third, the specific attributes of the product itself: its appearance, durability, viscosity, color, the guarantees it carries, etc. No doubt the contribution of physical attributes of the product to its brand image varies widely from product to product. Very often, it is the package rather than the product itself that make a major contribution to the perception of the product's physical attributes.

Fourth, the specific use to which most people put the product: e.g., is a particular paint used to paint barns, dog kennels, or living rooms? Sometimes a specific use is associated so strongly with a product that it dominates its image. For instance, the makers of Jell-O tried uncessfully to get consumers to think of this product as an elegant dessert. Consumers had become so used to thinking of Jell-O as a "shirtsleeves dessert" that they could not modify their impressions and begin to regard it as a luxury product. "If I have to spend so much time making a dessert," they said, "I might as well make a fancy dessert, not just Jell-O."

Studies in image research have established that the consumer does not consciously scrutinize the five main dimensions of a product's image (price, larger corporate entity, personality of user, product attributes, specific use) in forming his image of it. One or a combination of these dimensions is perceived by him first, and he may exclude the other dimensions. Inasmuch as the three schools of perception psychology are concerned with why individuals single out particular elements of a stimulus, they might help a marketer to understand how images are formed and what he might do to create favorable images for his products.

The central theme of the image approach is that the marketer must learn how consumers perceive his product and brand. Customers have been responding to brand images for a very long time without realizing it. At this late date, it seems pointless to question whether such an image is desirable; almost every company has one, be it good, bad, or indifferent. Marketers now have it within their power to employ selective procedures to heighten the consumer's perception of a brand's positive features and to minimize his perception of its negative features. The more enterprising marketers will modify the price, and other attributes of their product, in accordance with what is best for their brand's image in terms of their marketing goals.

Price is likely to be as important an image component as any of the others. The effect of price on the image varies. Its effect apparently depends largely on the product category. Price can be used to develop and sustain a brand or product image. One example comes from the highly competitive toilet-soap field, in which it is extremely difficult to achieve any clearly emergent image. The manufacturers of one soap (Dial) introduced it as a product with special qualities, which cost several times more than ordinary toilet soaps. After attracting a small group of consumers, the manufacturers then reduced the price progressively (from 49 cents to 13 cents); each price reduction apparently gave purchasers a feeling that they were getting a high-quality product at a bargain price. The original perception, probably reflecting the Gestalt principle of <u>incongruity</u> (the special effect on perception of a stimulus having contradictory or paradoxical components), centered around the very high price and attracted purchasers. The high price helped to establish a quality level, which then formed the core of the soap's image.

One study has demonstrated that the consumer's perception of certain products (e.g., floor wax, razor blades) is such that he associates a higher price with a higher-quality product; this is not true of other products (e.g., cooking sherry, moth flakes).[22] Thus, the price of a product must be consonant with other components of the image, or there will be a "cognitive dissonance," which may lead to a decline in sales. Image studies show that high price, up to some point, is usually associated with a more favorable image of a product than is low price. Of course, although a consumer may have a favorable image of a high-priced product, his financial circumstances may lead him to purchase a lower-image, low-priced product.

Situations in Which Seller and Buyer Misperceptions Are Incompatible

Many conflicts arise because the disputants have a different view of the situation under contention. In such instances, a mediator may sometimes resolve the disagreement by altering the perceptions of the person whose views are unrealistic. In many business situations, however, there are no mediators available to correct misperceptions; as a result, if the buyer and the seller persistently take a different view of the facts in any situation, one must anticipate constant conflict. Just such a conflict may exist when manufacturers sell through independent distributors.

Firms that distribute their products nationally often sell their output through independent distributors whose markets are essentially local. Local markets may vary widely in their competitiveness and in the form that competition takes; measures that prove successful in selling a brand of product in one market will fail in others; a price that is appropriate in one may be quite

---

[22]Harold J. Leavitt, "A Note on Some Experimental Findings about the Meanings of Price," <u>Journal of Business</u>, 27 (1954), 205-210.

out of place in another. Accordingly, national firms often require special prices for at least a few particularly competitive individual markets, as well as a national price schedule that will apply in all other markets.

Dispute is likely to arise as a result of pressure from local distributors for reduced prices. Almost every local distributor can cite, as justification for a price reduction, at least one other brand of product that is selling for less than he charges -- or whose distributor pays less than he does for the product. It is easy for him to press his demands, for he loses nothing if the request is granted. On the other hand, the manufacturer of the nationally distributed brand generally does not believe that the brand should necessarily sell for the lowest price paid in the market, for he thinks that the nationally advertised name of his product has some price value. He will expect his distributors to be able to sell the nationally known name for a price.

Also, whereas the local distributors will feel extremely threatened by local competitors who pay and charge less than they do, the national manufacturer will not feel equally threatened. Since his sales in that one market will represent a relatively small proportion of his total sales, he can afford to gamble with a high price more easily than the distributor can afford to live with such a price. Similarly, the manufacturer and distributor will possess different amounts of information about the local situation, and their perceptions will be colored accordingly.

As a result of these differences in perceptions of the "right price" for a product in a local market, one would expect to find frequent misperceptions and consequent disputes between manufacturers and their distributors. There certainly are many disputes between manufacturers and their distributors, and one finds heavy turnover among the distributors for most nationally distributed products. Of course, it is impossible to determine exactly how many of these disputes result from incompatible misperceptions. However, these incompatible misperceptions probably would continue even if the manufacturer were to establish his own local distributor organizations -- as many manufacturers have done; for most of the circumstances that create different perceptions when the distributor is an independent businessman also exist when he is an employee of the national manufacturing organization.

CHAPTER V

ATTITUDES AND PRICING

Like the preceding chapter, this one is divided into two sections: the first reviews the behavioral science literature dealing with the formation and change of attitudes; the second explains a few applications of these materials to pricing, and explores ways in which they significantly improve our understanding of price. Since the literature dealing with attitudes is enormous, the review of behavioral science findings about attitudes necessarily is severely compressed. The discussion of applications to pricing is similarly selective. Despite the abbreviated nature of this explanation of attitudes and their bearing upon price, it nevertheless does give a rough indication of the potential value of behavioral science findings to this special phase of marketing.

BEHAVIORAL SCIENCE FINDINGS ON ATTITUDES

Physical scientists have often had to posit the existence of something which was not directly accessible to inquiry and which only subsequently was shown to exist; similarly, social psychologists have postulated the existence of attitudes to explain many facets of human perception and behavior. An attitude is difficult to define precisely, because nobody has ever seen one, although many social scientists have studied, measured, and reported the effects of attitudes. For purposes of discussion, an attitude can be defined as a predisposition to behavior. The possession of one attitude rather than another, then, disposes a person to behave in a particular way. Although this concept of the attitude, as something underlying behavior, is quite abstract, it is possible to study and measure attitudes fairly accurately.

Most of us are not aware of our specific attitudes on any given subject until we are specifically asked about them, even though those attitudes may strongly affect our behavior. Attitudes are not necessarily unconscious, however, even though we cannot state them explicity without some prodding. Most of us have little occasion to take stock of our various attitudes; but when asked about our attitudes on specific subjects, we generally can express what they are.

The enormous range of attitudes that any individual holds can be seen in compilations like that of Cantril and Strunk,[1] who reported on the literally thousands of attitude surveys that have been made since the 1930s. Not only are attitudes toward traditional subjects like the tariff and capital punishment included in such compilations, but also attitudes toward matters like the current rate of income tax, sexual behavior, and the allowance that a ten-year-old child should get. Newspaper reports of attitude surveys, like those conducted by George Gallup or Elmo Roper, often convey a mistaken impression. The precise percentages in which they give the proportion of the public which holds a given attitude imply that attitudes can be measured precisely and are quite consistent. Actually, the same individual's attitudes on related subjects may be incompatible with one another. A person might believe simultaneously that school taxes should be lowered and that we should have better schools and more highly qualified teachers, even though taxes clearly would have to be increased if schools are to be improved. In a referendum on whether there should be an increase in taxes to pay for better schools, a person holding such views would have to resolve the inconsistency in one way or the other. For the most part, persons can hold contradictory attitudes without ever being forced to face their inconsistency.

Just as our endocrine glands maintain the body's internal equilibrium, by a process which physiologists call homeostasis, everyone apparently has an inner balancing mechanism that keeps disparate attitudes in harmony. In the body, one gland will increase or decrease its flow in response to an increase or decrease in the flow of another gland. Similarly, if a political figure whom a person admires takes a position which the same person dislikes, then the person will modify his attitudes in one direction or the other. He may think less of the candidate or he may modify his opinion on the issue. Some reconciliation of the two opinions, in all probability, will be attempted by the person's homeostatic-like attitude-balancing mechanism.

In some situations, behavior may be inconsistent with attitudes, but these generally are situations in which we lack complete control over our behavior. For example, the 1954 Supreme Court decision on desegregation meant that many southern white students would commingle with Negro students, even though the white students might be opposed to such commingling. However, this kind of discrepancy between attitude and behavior is unusual. The apparent conflict between the white students' attitudes and behavior toward Negro students can be explained by the consistency between the students' behavior and their attitudes toward observing laws.

---

[1]Hadley Cantril and Mildred Strunk, Public Opinion 1935-1946 (Princeton: Princeton University Press, 1947).

Attitudes are only partial determinants of behavior. Behavior is also affected by temperament, moods, opinions, physical states, and other factors, which are not always easy to distinguish from attitudes. Temperament is the expression of the person's activity level and is largely a reflection of basal metabolism and endocrine balance. It is mainly temperament that determines whether a person bounds cheerfully out of bed or requires three cups of coffee to awaken. A mood is a condition of temperament -- happy, elated, sad, ebullient -- which provides a framework for the expression of attitudes. A particular mood is not likely to change attitudes but will alter their expression and cause behavior to be somewhat inconsistent.[2] It is obvious that a shopper's mood when she enters a department store will influence her expressed attitudes toward specific products and her buying behavior.

An opinion is the expression of an attitude on a relatively concrete and narrow subject -- e.g., Do you think tariffs should be raised on imported bicycles? An opinion may reflect more than one attitude, and an attitude will generally be father to hundreds of specific opinions, just as it is responsible for many feelings and convictions.

Although the concept of the attitude is relatively complicated, its effect on human behavior in many practical situations is such that it is perhaps the most important single area of study and research in social psychology. If we are interested in how people will respond to a traffic light or whether they will buy a product, we must consider their attitudes. These will affect not only their behavior but their values and perceptions, and their interpretation of the behavior of others.

Formation of Attitudes

The process of acquiring an attitude is very subtle; rarely can a person explain accurately how any of his attitudes were acquired. Allport has suggested that there are four processes by which attitudes are likely to be formed: (1) integrating a number of similar experiences, (2) differentiating from general to specific situations, (3) unusual experiences, or (4) adopting attitudes from others.[3]

Integration of similar experiences. As an example of the first of these processes, an American soldier might have gone overseas in World War II without any specific attitudes toward Germans. As his unit moved into Germany and he met the natives, he would inevitably have specific experiences

---

[2]Patricia Kendall, Mood and Affect (Glencoe, Ill.: Free Press, 1956).

[3]Gordon W. Allport, "Attitudes," in Handbook of Social Psychology, ed. Carl Murchison (Worcester, Mass.: Clark University Press, 1935), pp. 798-844.

with them. Gradually, he would put together these experiences into an attitude toward Germans.

Differentiating from general to specific situations. Inferences from broad attitudes already held -- the second of Allport's processes - account for most of our narrow attitudes. Thus, if a person is asked his attitude toward women drivers, his answer may unconsciously reflect an underlying attitude that women in general are less competent or more careful than men. Someone else may dislike anything foreign and, when asked about the existentialist school of philosophy, will particularize this dislike and express negative attitudes toward existentialism because it is foreign. But the process by which the specific attitude individuates itself into awareness is not likely to be conscious, so that an individual is likely to respond to the specific question without consciously recalling the general underlying attitude that is parent to his answer.

Unusual experience. Unusual experiences constitute a third source of formation of attitudes. Reports of the collision between the liners "Andrea Doria" and "Stockholm" off Nantucket in the summer of 1956, for example, suggest that many passengers who had no specific attitudes toward Italians, or who had thought Italians were lazy and incompetent, developed very positive attitudes toward them based on the heroic behavior of the Italian crewmen of the "Andrea Doria."[4] If experiences involve outstanding examples of success or failure, they are particularly likely to create or alter attitudes.

Identification. The adoption of attitudes from others whom we admire or with whom we identify is a fourth and frequent basis of attitude formation. By identification we mean the desire of the individual to be like another person and the molding of his ego in line with this desire. One sees examples of this process in the elementary school students who adopt the attitudes of their teachers and sometimes begin to ape their teachers' costumes. Similarly, the high morale of the German troops, even after losing World War II, has been attributed mainly to their identification with their officers.[5] It has been shown that the political affiliations of people, by and large, are similar to those of their parents. Not only political but many other kinds of attitudes derive from parents, because of the great extent to which the growing child identifies with parents.

_____

[4]Paul Friedman and Louis Linn, "Some Psychiatric Notes on the Andrea Doria Disaster," American Journal of Psychiatry, 114 (1957), 426-432.

[5]Edward A. Shils and Morris Janowitz, "Cohesion and Disintegration in the Wehrmacht," Public Opinion Quarterly, 12 (1948), 300-315.

Personality. Another basis of attitude formation, not mentioned by Allport, is the incorporation of attitudes that make one's personality feel comfortable. Some attitudes are much more compatible with a person's personality than others. Indeed, to a great extent, our attitudes are our personality. Thus, individuals may have needs that make it important, in terms of their "personality economy," to hold particular attitudes. One study, for example, showed that the maintenance of specific attitudes toward the Soviet Union served a variety of very valuable purposes for the personalities of the individuals studied.[6] A number of studies have established this dimension of the "personal significance" of attitudes and have included such subjects as: Why do rumors spread?[7] Why did people believe the Orson Welles "Invasion from Mars" broadcast?[8] What is the "personal significance" of product categories like cigarettes and automobiles?[9] These studies have shown that a person's attitudes help to establish his identity. If one knows a person's predispositions to behavior -- his attitudes -- one knows a great deal about him and how he will behave. Similarly, if one knows the basic personality structure of an individual, he can forecast quite accurately the attitudes that individual will hold.

Social factors. Another major influence on attitudes is the general social class or group to which the individual belongs. Jews' attitudes toward eating food that is not "kosher" are derived from their social group.[10] Attitudes that are profoundly anchored in a social group are likely to be very meaningful to the individual. Kinsey has established that our attitudes toward even so central a phenomenon as sex are partially a function of our social class.[11] Perhaps the most poignant story in all of Kinsey's work is that of the lower-class prostitute who told the interviewer, after discussing a whole series of perversions in which she regularly engaged, that she did have one very

[6]Jerome S. Bruner, Robert W. White, and M. B. Smith, Opinions and Personality (New York: Wiley, 1955).

[7]Leon Festinger et al., "A Study of a Rumor," Human Relations, 1 (1948), 464-486.

[8]Hadley Cantril, The Invasion from Mars (Princeton: Princeton University Press, 1940).

[9]Cigarettes and Automobiles, What They Mean to Americans (Chicago: The Chicago Tribune, 1954).

[10]The Joseph Jacobs Organization (342 Madison Ave., New York) has published a number of pamphlets that give the details of kosher food taboos.

[11]Alfred C. Kinsey et al., Sexual Behavior in the Human Female (Philadelphia: Saunders, 1953).

embarrassing confession to make; it was that she slept "with no clothes on." In the lower-class circles from which she came, sleeping in the nude was simply not done, whereas it is very common in the upper classes. The class and social structure into which a person is born is, then, likely to create a variety of relatively specific and deep-rooted attitudes.

Dimensions of Attitudes

Attitudes have several dimensions by which they may be measured and described. These dimensions include direction, degree or intensity, salience, and the degree of public or private expression of the attitudes.

Direction. The direction of an attitude refers to whether one is for or against a fact, person, or situation. Are the emotional connotations of the attitude positive or negative? Will the individual tend to vote for or against a particular amendment? Will he tend to be friendly or unfriendly toward the new migrants? Does he or does he not like the New York Yankees? This dimension of attitude is easiest to measure and assess.

Degree. Another dimension of attitudes is the degree of intensity with which a person holds an attitude. Researchers usually measure this dimension by asking a respondent to rate how strongly he feels about a problem: e.g., "How strongly do you hold this opinion -- very strongly, fairly strongly, or don't you care much one way or the other?" Two people, for instance, might want the New York Yankees to win the professional baseball pennant, but they might hold this attitude with different degrees of intensity. Two people may have negative attitudes about Communism, but one may be a Marxist Socialist and the other a right-wing Republican. The Socialist's attitudes toward the economic doctrines of Communism are likely to be much less harsh than those of the right-wing Republican. When an attitude is strongly held, it can be called a conviction.

Salience. The salience of an attitude describes how central or peripheral a given attitude is to a person; it indicates the importance of an attitude to an individual. One's most salient ideas, as has been noted, are his personality, and are therefore relatively difficult to change -- although almost all can be changed under extreme circumstances. For example, attitudes toward parents, money, the opposite sex, and religion are likely to be far more salient than attitudes toward television commercials or traffic regulations.

Degree of public expression. The circumstances under which a person is willing to express an attitude may be considered a separate dimension. People will be willing to express some of their opinions publicly but will make others known only in confidence; also, in their public statements they may actually misrepresent their attitudes, because they may feel obliged, for whatever reason, to conceal their true views.

Changing Attitudes

Students of attitudes are especially concerned with how they can be changed and modified. Some attitudes may not be consonant with our objectives; consequently, it is of the greatest importance to know whether and how such attitudes can be altered.

Some kinds of attitudes are not likely to change. Attitudes that have a relatively high degree of salience are difficult to change. People who identify strongly with a group -- athletes, "beatniks," Ivy Leaguers, etc. -- are not likely to adopt attitudes that conflict with the group's norms. Similarly, attitudes that have been expressed publicly are not as changeable as those held in private.

Some kinds of attitudes are amendable to change. An attitude is more likely to be changed if the stimuli making for change are repeated. It is also more likely to be changed if whatever lies behind the attitude is modified, whether the underlying substratum of the attitude be some factual information or some component of the individual's personality, or of his culture or society. An attitude is relatively likely to be changed if those who are persuading the individual to change it seem to share other attitudes with him.

Attitudes can be changed in a number of ways, many of which are similar to the procedures by which the attitudes were acquired in the first place: integration of similar experiences, differentiating from general to specific situations, unusual experiences, identification, personality consonance with the attitudes, or social factors. Specifically designed attitude-changing communications may also be responsible for a change.

Even relatively salient attitudes are subject to change. Within one generation, our attitudes toward the Japanese people have changed sharply. After Pearl Harbor and during World War II, the Japanese were regarded as wily, cruel, and cunning adversaries. After 1945, they were generally believed to be meek and docile. By the late 1950s they were seen as forceful equals of Americans. Each of these attitude changes was related to some shift in American-Japanese relations. Another well-known example of attitude change is found in America's attitude toward the Russians. Before World War II, they were believed to be hostile and unfriendly and relatively backward technologically. During World War II, they were regarded as friendly, although their mastery of modern technology was still believed to be quite poor. With the cold war of the post-1945 period, they were once again regarded as unfriendly. With Sputnik, the Russians were no longer believed to be technologically backward. These attitude changes were facilitated by changing international events, even though, as in the case of the Japanese, each attitude was salient at the time it was held.

There is general agreement that an attitude in a state of flux, or on a subject about which there is little previous information or experience, is the easiest to change. [12] Thus, we might expect that it would be easier to change attitudes toward Martians or lemmings than toward Frenchmen or women. This principle was illustrated in one study of attitudes toward the two candidates for governor of New York in 1958. [13] It was found that voters' attitudes toward Nelson Rockefeller shifted substantially after they had seen him on television, whereas attitudes toward Governor Averell Harriman did not shift much after his television appearances. This was explained on the basis of Harriman's being a familiar personality toward whom attitudes had already formed; whereas, because there were less specific attitudes toward Rockefeller, they could be easily swayed.

Influence of group membership on attitude change. World War II supplied much invaluable data about attitude change. The army's research program on attitude change in soldiers was a massive effort. [14] It sharpened our knowledge of the effects of media on attitudes and the role of reference groups in attitude change. Reference groups are groups with which a person identifies or aspires to identify. The army research program afforded unparalleled opportunities for experimentation with different approaches to modifying attitudes. It yielded data on the persistence of attitude change. Other opportunities for research during the war occurred when the federal government became interested in getting women to buy more of the generally ignored kinds of animal organs, like brains and kidneys. [15] As a series of experiments clearly demonstrated, it was easier to change the attitudes of women toward the unfamiliar food when they discussed the pros and cons among themselves and decided, on the basis of group discussion, to try the food than when experts in nutrition gave them well-documented lectures on the desirability of using the newer foods. This experience supports the conclusion that a group decision is likely to be relatively more effective in activating attitude change than is a decision handed down by an authority figure.

The power of group membership in achieving attitude change, even in the face of considerable resistance to change, can be seen in the development of Alcoholics Anonymous. The feeling of belonging to a larger group is perhaps

[12] Charles Winick, "How People Perceived 'The Mad Bomber,'" Public Opinion Quarterly, 25 (1961), in press.

[13] Television and the Political Candidate, a study conducted by the Cunningham and Walsh Company (260 Madison Avenue, New York, 1959).

[14] Samuel A. Stouffer et al., The American Soldier, 4 vol. (Princeton: Princeton University Press, 1948-1950).

[15] The Problem of Changing Food Habits: Report of the Committee on Food Habits, 1941-1943 (Washington, D.C., National Research Council, 1943).

the major therapeutic agent that Alcoholics Anonymous contributes toward a change in the individual's attitude toward drinking. Membership in Alcoholics Anonymous has helped many problem drinkers to stop drinking, after all other methods have proved unsuccessful.

Even an attitude toward something as personal as one's choice of alcoholic beverage may shift when an individual changes his work-group affiliations. A hobo, sitting on a park bench sipping sherry from a demijohn in a brown paper bag, is likely to modify his attitudes and begin drinking beer when he becomes a workman. Promoted to be an office worker, he may begin to prefer rye whiskey. Once he becomes a junior executive, he may again modify his attitudes and begin drinking Scotch. If he is promoted to top management, his attitudes are likely to be further modified, and he may again be drinking sherry -- although doubtless a brand different from the hobo's. The individual's attitude toward drinking will not change automatically with the assumption of each of these social roles. Rather, there will be a process of identification with each new group; and the resulting pattern of behavior requires a shift in attitude. In each group, the person's new friends have attitudes to which he must adapt himself; and such factors, along with the new group identification, make the attitude shift easier to achieve.

Prestige suggestion as a method of modifying attitudes. During the 1930s and 1940s a major direction of research in attitude change was the study of prestige suggestion, or the effect of knowing that a particular person holds a specific attitude or has created a particular work of art. In one classical study, Sherif asked his subjects to rank various writers: Conrad, Dickens, Poe, Scott, and Stevenson.[16] Some weeks later, he gave the subjects various literary passages, each attributed to a different member of this group of writers, and asked the subjects to rank the literary merit of the passages. The subjects' ranking of the passages generally coincided with their previously expressed ranking of the authors -- although all the passages were actually by the same writer (Stevenson). Clearly, the subjects had evaluated the passages in terms of their underlying attitudes toward their favorite and not-so-favorite authors.

In other studies, students' attitudes toward various current issues and political leaders were established.[17] Some time later, they were shown statements that the political leaders had made on the issues in question. After a period of time, the students were again asked the same questions that had been used to determine their original attitudes. In general, the principle of prestige suggestion operated relatively clearly: the subjects had modified

---

[16]Muzafer Sherif, "An Experimental Study of Stereotypes," Journal of Abnormal and Social Psychology, 29 (1935), 371-375.

[17]Solomon E. Asch, "The Doctrine of Suggestion, Prestige, and Imitation in Social Psychology," Psychological Review, 55 (1948), 5-20.

their attitudes so that they corresponded with the attitudes attributed to the political leaders whom they admired.

In the last ten years, numerous studies of prestige suggestion have concentrated on the role of the opinion leader (the person in a group to whom others look for advice on a particular issue) as a major factor in changing attitudes and behavior. This opinion leader has also been called an "influential."[18] He has been shown to influence doctors in selecting prescription drugs;[19] farmers in learning new procedures of agriculture;[20] women in selecting stores to buy in, movies to see, and dresses to buy; and in many other situations.[21] Such studies have demonstrated that prestige suggestion can operate from members of one's own social circle or work group. In addition, they have underscored the importance of the means whereby one receives an attitude-changing communication: it is more likely to be successful if it comes from an opinion leader in one's own group than if it comes from media. A group of Yale psychologists have extensively demonstrated that attitude change is partially a function of the credibility and perceived motivations of the communicator.[22]

APPLICATION OF BEHAVIORAL SCIENCE MATERIALS ON ATTITUDES TO PRICING

Applications to pricing of the concepts and findings reviewed will now be explored. An exhaustive list of applications will not be attempted; instead, a few prevalent attitudes, some held by those who set price and others held by customers, will be discussed to indicate how an understanding of attitudes can be of genuine value for all who establish price or who wish to understand the pricing process.

---

[18] The Influentials (Philadelphia, Saturday Evening Post, 1956).

[19] Herbert Menzel and Elihu Katz, "Social Relation and Innovation in the Medical Profession: The Epidemiology of a New Drug," Public Opinion Quarterly, 19 (1955-1956), 337-352.

[20] How Farm People Accept New Ideas (Ames: Iowa State College, Agricultural Extension Service, Nov. 1955), Special Report No. 15.

[21] Elihu Katz and Paul F. Lazarsfeld, Personal Influence (Glencoe, Ill.: Free Press, 1955).

[22] Carl I. Hovland, Irving L. Janis, and Harold H. Kelley, Communication and Persuasion (New Haven: Yale University Press, 1953).

Attitudes Prevalent Among Price-Setters

What attitudes are held by most business executives that are likely to affect their price decisions? What is the effect of these attitudes? Do they militate for or against price changes? Do they lead executives to charge more or less than they otherwise would? Since such attitudes are often unconscious, do they impair the ability of these executives to make efficient price decisions?

No systematic formal study has been made of attitudes which are shared by executives and influence their pricing decisions. Consequently, it is necessary to make inferences based on the extant literature and personal experience. Two attitudes that apparently affect many price decisions will be discussed briefly, for purposes of illustration, in order to explore whether most price decisions are substantially different than they would be if executives did not hold these attitudes.

First of all, most price-setters seem to believe that prices should move parallel to costs. This attitude represents almost a pricing formula. Indeed, according to studies that have been made of industrial pricing methods, the most commonly employed method of establishing price maintains a constant margin between some base cost and price.[23] This method is variously termed cost-plus or average-cost pricing.

Cost-plus pricing prevails despite the demonstrable fact that it rarely will yield maximum profit for the firm and is incompatible with the widely cited "law of supply and demand." This cost method of pricing ignores demand considerations altogether! It probably is employed, despite its inconsistency with economic doctrine, at least partly because of the power of the attitude that prices should be based upon cost alone.

It is easy to explain much anomalous price behavior by this attitude. For example, some businesses raise prices during recession, despite a decline in sales of their product. Sometimes the rise in price is associated with an increase in wage rates won in a labor negotiation, or with a rise in raw-material prices, or with a rise in overhead costs per unit due to a decline in the firm's rate of capacity utilization.

Conversely, in innumerable cases businessmen have maintained prices despite a rise in replacement cost. It is still almost the rule for firms selling at retail not to mark up merchandise on their shelves, when the price of the merchandise has risen, until they themselves purchase new merchandise at the higher price. Their behavior seems to reflect the attitude that prices should

---

[23]National Industrial Conference Board, "Pricing Practices of American Enterprise," Business Record, Sept. 1958.

move parallel to costs -- rather than that they be set in order to obtain a maximum long-run profit for the enterprise.

This attitude is not held by business executives alone. Consumers share it; consequently, they seem to accept -- almost cheerfully -- increases in price associated with higher costs to the producer. Similarly, government officials in public pronouncements imply that businessmen are ignoring their civic responsibility if they raise prices beyond the rise in their costs, but have every right to recover all increases in price that they must pay.

As a result, it is practically impossible to explain price behavior or to predict the behavior of one's competitors and regulatory agencies unless one recognizes and attaches heavy weight to this attitude. Similarly, one cannot understand the operations of the United States economy (and most other industrial economies, where similar attitudes prevail) without taking this dominant attitude into account.

The attitude that prices should vary directly with costs has spawned many related and widespread attitudes. One holds that each item in a firm's entire line of products should "stand on its own feet" and "carry its own weight." As a result of this attitude, items that do not cover their "accounting" costs are dropped -- even though they may greatly enhance the attractiveness of the entire line, contribute to covering overhead, and add to total profit. Also, this attitude militates against setting prices in a way that increases the profitability of an entire product line by accepting a very low price for one or a few selected items in the line.

Another significant and prevalent attitude, which is closely related to the attitude that prices should move parallel to costs, is what might be termed "public-utility-type thinking." This is the orientation that businessmen are entitled only to a "reasonable return on their investment"; consequently, even when they have an opportunity to command a very high price -- because of a shortage, exceptional product features, or the like -- they should not "take advantage of the situation" to demand a high price. Indeed, this attitude, as held by many businessmen and consumers alike, dictates that sellers should add a fairly uniform margin to all products they sell and that this margin should not be changed markedly over time. Many otherwise strange price phenomena -- particularly "grey markets" -- can be understood more readily if one takes account of attitudes like these, which may underlie the decisions of executives responsible for setting price.

A second major attitude prevalent among price-setters is that <u>management should "do something!" when sales decline</u>. Business executives, like most other groups, have a conception of their jobs and of themselves to which they attempt to adhere. Among the ingredients likely to be found in an executive's self-image is the attitude that he should be a man of action and deal quickly with difficulties as they arise; he should be resolute and prepared to take the consequences of his decisions. With this kind of general attitude among executives, one is likely to find price behavior that cannot be explained as a rational pursuit of self-interest or maximum profit for the firm.

There are many situations in which businessmen take price action when inaction would clearly be a wiser course. Such examples are especially plentiful during periods of declining sales. When sales fall throughout a market, due to broad economic forces that affect all rival firms more or less equally, it would rarely benefit any one firm to reduce its prices if all of its rivals would follow suit: all the firms would ordinarily sell essentially the same amount they would have sold had they retained the higher price, but would receive less for their product; and, when demand revived, they would have difficulty in raising prices back to their previous levels. Nevertheless, price reductions are extremely common under such circumstances -- even in industries where customers, who have been offered a price reduction by a source they do not patronize regularly, are able to obtain a similar price reduction from their present supplier. It is very difficult to explain this behavior without taking account of the tendency of executives to regard inaction -- especially with regard to price -- as perhaps the most difficult course of action for them.[24]

Attitudes Among Customers

To understand the source and power of most customer attitudes toward price, it is necessary to understand their attitudes toward money itself. The strongest attitudes that customers carry to the purchase situation probably relate to money itself. Their attitudes toward particular numerical prices, differentials in price for different brands of the same product, changes in price, etc., are often the major explanation for customer behavior; these, however, seem less salient than their attitudes toward money and ordinarily reflect those attitudes quite directly.

Attitudes toward money. Since virtually everyone beyond early child-hood buys some things, when one speaks of "customer attitudes" he is discussing the attitudes of almost everyone in the society under consideration. In the United States, and almost certainly in all other highly industrialized economies, most persons have extremely strong feelings about money.

Psychoanalysts have helped us to understand the great strength of most peoples' feelings about money and of the attitudes that reflect these

---

[24] For a fairly detailed consideration of this phenomenon in the steel industry, see Alfred R. Oxenfeldt, Industrial Pricing and Market Practices) (Englewood Cliffs, N.J.: Prentice-Hall, 1957), pp. 526-528.

feelings.[25] The salience and strength of these feelings and attitudes partially derive from their having been formed in very early childhood. Certainly, the average person's first contact with money often comes when he learns that money is one reason for his not being able to gratify his whims or desires. It generally takes place at an extremely early age -- long before he is capable of understanding the realistic significance of money. In even the most pros- perous households, money considerations are cited to the very young child as a major reason for his not wasting or destroying things and as one reason for his not having everything that takes his fancy. Thus, at a very early age, the child comes to regard money as something that is even bigger and more power- ful than his parents and something that has almost as much capacity as they do to satisfy his wants.

Another reason for money's importance is that it is frequently used as a reward for children by adults. Especially in the minds of young children, who do not understand the true significance of money, its status as both a reward and a goal gives it great emotional impact and accentuates its power.

Money generates attitudes of great strength for yet other reasons. In many homes, it is a source of tension that is ill-disguised from even young children and is often consciously communicated to older ones. This tension may arise because the family income is limited or the income-earner's employ- ment is insecure; or it may result from the divergent standards of expenditure of the individual parents. These circumstances combine to accentuate the emotionalism which parents feel toward money, and which they communicate to their children.

Despite the rough similarity in the circumstances under which most individuals form their earliest attitudes toward money, there is very great divergence in the specific content of those attitudes. For example, some in- dividuals are miserly and others are extravagant; some make a fetish of careful management and accounting for expenditure, while others value greatly the ability to be casual about expenditure. However, despite wide individual differences in fundamental attitudes toward money, there are very few people whose attitudes toward money lack great salience. One can distinguish some attitudes that strongly affect very large numbers of customers and are quite relevant to their reactions toward price, price differentials, and price changes. Other attitudes -- such as the attitude toward money as the best index of "success" or "brains" -- are no doubt extremely important in explaining human behavior, but are less directly relevant to an understanding of consumer behavior with respect to price. A few of these attitudes will be mentioned and described briefly in order to indicate their relevance to price and to demon- strate that it is not possible to explain consumer behavior fully or set prices effectively without taking cognizance of their content and their power.

---

[25]Otto Fenichel, Psychoanalytic Theory of Neurosis (New York: Norton, 1945), pp. 281-283.

Attitude toward transactions as "battles of wits." The author of
Ecclesiastes in the Old Testament may have gone a bit too far when he ex-
claimed "Vanity of vanities; all is vanity," but it is obvious that almost everyone usually desires to convey a good impression of himself. Almost everyone
has a homeostatic attitudinal balancing mechanism, which enables him to hold
as high an opinion of himself as possible. Adults, and more especially
parents, must recognize the purchase function as one of their important roles
in the family; to make ill-advised purchases, or to pay substantially more than
was necessary, thus represents ineptitude -- and may even inflict injury on
other members of the family. Even more important perhaps, it may signify
personal "failure" and may damage one's self-esteem.

If challenged, most people become very "defensive" about their purchases. They are likely to resist the implication that they overpaid or mis-
judged the quality of their purchase. If they have clearly obtained poor value,
they may seek a scapegoat. Generally they blame the seller, accusing him of
misrepresenting, acting in poor faith, or something similar. They consider
good purchasing (and thus obtaining good value for their money) to be "a
matter of principle" and "an end in itself"; their purchase behavior cannot,
therefore, be viewed solely in realistic and substantive terms. On substantive
grounds, it may not appear to be sufficiently important for a customer of
moderate income to walk several blocks to save 11 cents on a $1.00 purchase.
However, as a symbol of "success" and as a mark of virtue, the extra effort
will seem warranted to many and actually obligatory to some.

Little differences in price are likely to seem major items to most consumers, for the reasons discussed. Where product quality is demonstrably
the same (as where the same model of the same brand of the same product
sold at two stores is in question), a great barrier exists for most consumers if
price differs even slightly. They require a justification for paying the higher
price -- and, for the large majority, it does not seem to suffice that they will
save themselves some time or effort by paying the higher price. One finds
many extreme examples of unrealistic behavior that can be explained only by
highly salient attitudes toward money, combined with the attitude that a
person reveals his intelligence and diligence by the way he makes purchases.
Wealthy women who drive their limousines thirty miles through heavy traffic
to save 79 cents (although they are likely to speak of it as 25 per cent) are
not freaks by any means. They, and less extreme types, make up a sizable
proportion of those who patronize discount houses and who patronize "regular
sales" at all retail shops.

Attitude that waste is shameful, if not sinful. The United States is
identified by many Europeans as a nation of waste. Thus, although Europeans
have long regarded it as "wrong" to leave food on a plate when one has finished eating, in the United States only "crude" ill-mannered persons leave
their plates absolutely bare. Indeed, the acceleration of waste has come to

be viewed as a major American social contribution; and some marketing specialists proclaim that it is a virtual necessity for the continued prosperity of many
industries, if not the entire economy. Vance Packard, who has been highly
critical of those who influence the consumer to buy more or different things,
has hit this problem head-on and inspired further discussion of the subject in
his The Waste Makers.[26] Nonetheless, most persons in the United States
absorb some ascetic and "puritanical" attitudes that are most inhospitable to
waste. To destroy property or to use much when little would suffice is regarded
as categorically wrong in the attitude systems of most adults in the United
States. Similarly, to spend more than one needs to spend may also be regarded
as a categorical wrong and an unnecessary waste. Thus, the stigma attaching
to waste, reinforcing the attitude that purchases involve a battle of wits, makes
most consumers sensitive to the "fairness" of their purchase price; in particular, they are extremely sensitive to differences in price for the same brand of
item in different retail shops.

Price assumes particular importance in an economy where brands, especially national ones, assure consumers that quality is uniform among different
items of the same brand. Even though service and convenience should realistically figure in their calculations, many consumers tend to think and say that
they are getting the same thing when they obtain the same brand and model of
a given item. As a result, they tend to measure the "success" of any purchase
by comparing the price they paid with what other customers pay or what other
stores charge for the same item, rather than how the item compares in value
for them with other things they might have purchased with those funds or with
the value to them of holding those extra funds. In other words, consumers need
assurance that they cannot buy the same item for less elsewhere - far more
than they must be assured they need that item more than any other of equal cost.
The consumer is not very vulnerable to being proved "wasteful" or foolish if he
buys what he could very well have done without.

Conclusions

As we survey these applications of behavioral science material on attitudes, what have we said that is new? What conclusions for action can we
draw that are different from those already accepted by market practitioners
and teachers?

Cost-plus pricing has been a recognized fact for centuries; and price
theorists, most of them very reluctantly, have acknowledged its existence.
Some writers have even associated its prevalence with an attitude held by the
public at large. Similarly, almost every seller recognizes the sensitivity of
his customers to being overcharged, and all claim to charge a "fair price";

[26]Vance Packard, The Waste Makers (New York: David McKay, 1960).

indeed, most retailers actively or implicitly match the prices charged by competitors. Thus, behavioral science does not tell us anything about what happens that we did not know before. It does, however, explain why these things happen and it provides suggestions about what must be done.

Since cost-plus pricing rests upon a strongly held attitude, the practice will not be changed without first changing the attitude. Even if it were possible to destroy cost-plus pricing itself, the same results would be achieved by a different route as long as the basic attitude remains. Therefore, the only way to depart from cost-plus pricing would be to vest responsibility for pricing with persons whose biases run counter to these attitudes. Specifically, one might divest accountants and controllers of pricing responsibility and place it in the hands of sales persons who are not likely to ignore demand considerations.

Similarly, the strength of most customers' attitudes about money, and the expression of these attitudes in their reactions to price, contains implied suggestions for action. When a seller encounters an attitude that is so firmly held and deeply rooted, he cannot hope to change it; he must adapt to it. He must claim to provide good value and to charge prices in line with other vendors' prices. He cannot hope to persuade many customers to pay him a premium for the added convenience of not seeking out the source charging the lowest price. This is not to say that retailers cannot attract a tiny group of customers by almost any appeal, but a seller takes on a large and unnecessary burden when he fights against rather than reconciles himself to such a strong attitude system.

CHAPTER VI

GROUP MEMBERSHIP AND PRICING

Persons who establish price for business firms generally do so as members of one or more groups. Behavioral science has established that group memberships strongly affect human behavior. It therefore seems fitting to investigate whether pricers are affected by their group memberships in the discharge of their pricing responsibilities and, if so, whether that effect is beneficial or disadvantageous to the firm. In particular, we would want to discover the typical effect and the process by which it occurs. Such knowledge should make pricers more efficient by helping to identify group influences and to suggest appropriate corrections for those that are undesirable. Also, it should enable executives who supervise pricers to take steps to minimize the unfortunate effects of their subordinates' group memberships: for example, they might select for the task of pricing someone who can withstand certain kinds of group influences, or they may decide that prices should be set by a committee rather than by an individual. Since group influences might divert a pricer from pursuing his company's pricing objectives, awareness of their sources and nature should be of considerable value.

BEHAVIORAL SCIENCE FINDINGS ON GROUPS

Data on the influence of group memberships derive from many studies of small groups in the laboratory of the social psychologist, from studies of military groups, and from studies of voluntary groups. There has also been considerable field work on interpersonal relations within industrial groups. Virtually no information has been collected systematically, however, about the effects of group memberships on persons who set price. It will therefore be necessary to infer the relevance of the behavioral science findings to the pricing situation. Although the application of material from other fields creates the risk of overgeneralization; one incurs an even greater risk of error if he ignores this body of evidence altogether.

The possible errors of overgeneralization are compounded by the variety of sources from which information about groups is obtained: studies in group dynamics, social psychology, sociology, the military, industrial morale, socialization, ethnic attitudes, and other fields -- all deal with related but different dimensions of social behavior. Unfortunately, there exists no body of commonly accepted data or conclusions about how groups behave and how individuals are influenced by group membership. Instead, one can draw upon a number of insights from each of many disciplines; these partly conflict, but mostly reinforce one another.

Importance of Group Membership on Human Development

Introductory texts on human behavior used to discuss the significance of "feral man." ("Feral" is the name given to humans who have been raised by animals or have somehow survived away from contact with a human group.) Feral man was important in the early days of psychology because he was used to prove that a large part of human development was the result of nature rather than nurture. However, recent researches indicate that there is insufficient evidence to substantiate generalizations about feral man. All of the earlier cases of feral man have been shown to be either untrue, exaggerated, or based on overenthusiastic travelers' reports. After careful investigation, not one case has been authenticated.

By discarding the feral man concept, behavioral scientists have underscored the absolute necessity of group memberships for human development. It can be established that every person actually belongs to many formal and informal groups; that he also regards himself as belonging to many groups, although these may not be the same as the groups to which he actually belongs; and that he is likely to aspire to membership in some groups to which he admittedly does not belong. Much evidence can be adduced to show that human behavior varies with group membership -- whether real or imagined -- and with group-membership aspirations. Quite as important: for behavior to alter substantially, apparently people must view themselves as having shifted from one group to another.

When behavioral scientists speak of groups, they refer to two or more people who interact with one another. In this sense, families, clubs, professional societies, PTA groups, etc., are organized or formal groups; informal groups are those composed of "liberals," "beatniks," "rugged individualists," "intellectuals," etc. Some of these groups are small and some are large; some meet face to face, others do not. Among those who do meet, some meet far more frequently and for longer times than others. All, however, consist of two or more people who interact with one another. (Interaction can be defined as behavior that involves mutual awareness between or among people.)

When people interact with one another, they feel, think, perceive, and act differently than they would if they were not interacting with others. In short, group membership influences a person's perceptions, attitudes, emotions, thought processes, the expression of his personality, his aspirations, and, of course, his actions. Often, the influence of group membership on behavior is greater than all other factors, and provides the most useful basis for forecasting human behavior.

In describing someone to another person, we generally identify him by his formal and informal group membership. They are almost as much a characteristic of a person as his physical appearance and possessions. In psychological terms and as bases for explaining behavior, they are probably far more illuminating than most obvious and measurable characteristics. The importance of group memberships in explaining human behavior may become clearer if one recognizes their close relationship to the concept of self-image. Almost everyone regards himself as a particular kind of person, and his definition of this kind of person includes the types of people with whom he associates -- i.e., the groups to which he belongs.

Every member of a group is not influenced in the same way or to the same extent by group membership. How much a person's experience and behavior may be affected is determined largely by the nature of his relationships with other members of the group, his position in the hierarchical structure of the group, and by the kind of behavior that group members expect from someone in his position. Thus, the particular influence of group membership on any individual's behavior depends upon that individual's status and role in the group.

As already indicated, one must consider the groups to which the person does in fact belong (for, at least subconsciously, he will have some recognition of reality), the groups to which he consciously believes that he belongs, and those to which he aspires to belong. These groups are known as reference groups, and -- together with the concepts of status, role, and leadership -- they go far to explain the effects of group membership on individual behavior.

Reference Groups

A number of different disciplines have effectively employed the concept of the reference group in studies of group influences. The concept has developed because of the need to explain the obvious fact that not all of the groups to which a person belongs affect his behavior, and that some affect his behavior more than others. Moreover, a person's feelings, thoughts, and actions may be affected most by groups to which he does not actually belong. Ordinarily, an individual's attitudes and actions are influenced to some degree by the groups of which he is an actual member, i.e., by his membership groups. Sometimes, however, the individual may actually be a member of one group but may identify himself psychologically with a different group - his reference group. In such a case, the group to which he belongs will probably have little influence on his behavior, whereas the group with which he identifies is likely to have a great influence, as in the "status seekers" of popular literature. Although a person's reference group is usually his actual membership group as well, this is frequently not so.

The individual's behavior, then, is more likely to be influenced by the reference group with which he is psychologically affiliated than by the group of which he is formally a member. To understand the behavior of any person or group, one must therefore take into account the concept of the reference group.

In the years since Hyman coined the term "reference group" in 1942,[1] perhaps the most successful use so far made of the concept of the reference group in behavioral science research is in the studies, by Stouffer and his associates,[2] of attitudes of soldiers in World War II. Many of the important attitudes of the soldiers were found to be mediated by the soldiers' constant comparisons of themselves with one or more of three groups of soldiers: (1) those with whom they were in actual association (friends); (2) those in the same status or social category (other sergeants); and (3) those in a different status or social category (combat soldiers compared with noncombat soldiers). Each of these three reference groups played some part in the development of the soldiers' attitudes.

The concept of relative deprivation has been employed to explain this process of constant comparison with others.[3] This concept refers to the extent to which peoples' attitudes depend on the groups with which they compare themselves, and the extent to which they feel that others who are equally deserving are or are not in a comparable situation. For example, a married man inducted into the army may question why he was inducted, because he perceives his situation within two other frames of reference: undrafted married men still in civilian life, and unmarried men who were drafted but whose induction did not call for comparable sacrifice. Relative to these two groups, the soldier may feel that he is relatively deprived. This phenomenon is generalizable into many nonmilitary situations because of the widespread tendency of individuals, in many different situations, to compare themselves with particular groups. Any persons who are involved in attempts to change the behavior of others are perforce required to think about the reference group with which the recommended behavior will be identified, and to determine whether there will be a feeling of relative deprivation associated with it.

Other valuable studies of group identification have been conducted in prisons.[4] Studies of prison communities have shown that some prisoners

[1]Herbert Hyman, The Psychology of Status, Archives of Psychology, 1942, No. 269. "Reflections on Reference Groups," Public Opinion Quarterly, 24 (1960), 383-396.

[2]Samuel A. Stouffer et al., The American Soldier. 4 vol. (Princeton: Princeton University Press, 1948-1950).

[3]Robert K. Merton, Social Theory and Social Structure (Glencoe, Ill.: Free Press, 1957), pp. 225-386.

[4]D. Clemmer, The Prison Community (Boston: Christopher, 1940).

completely lose their outside identities and associate themselves with the prison group. Other prisoners identify with groups outside prison and do not become integrated into the social world of the prison; their bases for self-evaluation refer to norms outside the prison group. A third group of prisoners identifies itself with the reference group of prisoners in some ways and with the reference group of the outside world in other ways.

People generally change their reference groups only very gradually. Thus, a nurse who has gone to medical school will almost never be accepted as a physician by the hospital where she was a nurse. Moreover, in spite of her M.D. degree, she herself probably will still identify with the nursing-force reference group. Often, she must go to another hospital in order to avoid this identification.[5]

Role and Status

The concept of role has occupied a central position in social science almost from its very beginning, but it has undergone considerable development. At first, role was used to denote the actions that society expects of persons in particular situations.[6] Thus, it was said that society expects a doctor's behavior to be different from a farmer's, a farmer's behavior to be different from an unskilled industrial worker's, etc. After a time, however, it became clear that society at large does not have common expectations about the behavior of most groups. Instead, society is composed of many segments, each of which may have different expectations. For example, a majority of the general public may expect particular behavior from doctors, but the public's expectations would be at variance with those of nurses. Similarly, hospital administrators and public health authorities expect doctors to behave in a particular way, at least in their associations with them; and these expectations are different from those of the general public and the nurses. The notion of role set takes account of the diverse roles played by an individual as a result of membership in a single group. Inasmuch as individuals belong to many groups and many of these groups involve a whole set of roles, a substantial proportion of human behavior is influenced by group membership.

Some roles are more pervasive and less limited than others. A priest's role, for example, is clearly at the core of everything he does. A fireman is likely to doff his role along with his uniform. One expects a great difference in the behavior of priests and firemen, basically because of their different group memberships and the roles expected of persons in those groups.

---

[5]Charles Winick, "The Hospital as a Social System," New York State Nurse, 26 (1955), 9-13.

[6]Ralph Linton, The Study of Man (New York: Appleton-Century, 1936).

Defined formally, a role is composed of behavior patterns that constitute a meaningful unit and are considered appropriate to: (1) a given status in society, (2) an informally defined position in interpersonal relations, or (3) identification with a particular value. Role refers to behavior -- a person enacts a role. Status denotes position; it thus refers to a condition rather than to action. A role is the dynamic component of a status. Each role has status and each status implies a role.

Role is a useful concept for understanding social behavior because it is an interactional concept. A role is partly cultural, partly personal, and partly situational. Although most people are not consciously and formally aware of the roles they play, nevertheless they act out the behavior that these roles require.

An example of conscious role behavior can be found in Komarovsky's study of role behavior in college girls.[7] She found that the girls were uncertain about whether to play the role of the intelligent student or the expected feminine role of dependence and inferiority. Nearly half of the girls studied deliberately "played dumb" on dates, because they felt this was proper role behavior. Other examples of role behavior are seen in the college student who joins a fraternity and is subjected to the tremendous pressures of the fraternity for conformity to certain kinds of behavior that may have been quite foreign to him. The "pledge" in a fraternity may feel obliged to do things that he actively dislikes doing. To take another extreme example, concentration-camp inmates assuming the involuntary role of prisoners changed not only their attitudes and behavior, but even their personality and emotional tone.[8] Studies have shown that junior executives joining corporations and adopting the role of the executive often modify their usual personality manifestations very markedly, as a result of their becoming members of the corporation "family."[9]

Status has an even more obvious effect on behavior. Think of a private in the ranks of an army platoon, complaining bitterly about the noncommissioned and commissioned officers and perhaps even "goldbricking" and doing as little work as possible. The same soldier, once appointed a corporal or sergeant, is likely to begin to complain about the privates in the platoon and

---

[7]Mirra Komarovsky, "Cultural Contradictions and Sex Roles," American Journal of Sociology, 52 (1946), 184-189.

[8]Bruno Bettelheim, "Individual and Mass Behavior in Extreme Situations," Journal of Abnormal and Social Psychology, 38 (1943), 417-452.

[9]William H. Whyte, Jr., The Organization Man (New York: Simon and Schuster, 1956).

their "goldbricking." This process has been recorded by Harold Peat [10] for World I and by Marion Hargrove for World War II. [11]

Leadership

Another important concept that explains the effects of group membership upon individual behavior is leadership. Most groups have leaders, and these persons strongly influence group functioning. The leader of a group helps to establish and express the goals and activities of the group. Just what the leader does will vary with the type of group being led, as well as with his personality and situation. The leader, however, exercises certain specific functions and has certain qualities in almost every group situation. Among these functions and qualities are: coordinating the activities that give the group its qualities of groupness, planning and establishing policy, being specially well informed, representing the members of the group in contacts with others, arbitrating internal group relationships, representing a paradigm of behavior for other members of the groups, and verbalizing the group's ideals. [12] Thus the leader of a group assumes a special status, which implies a particular set of roles different from those of nonleaders in the same group. [13] Indeed, the leader helps to define the roles of other members of his group, and to assign status to them.

Observation by sociologists of groups in offices, factories, communities, corporations, and business conferences have provided rich sources of data on leadership. [14] This tradition of observation is almost as old as sociology itself. Shortly after the turn of the century, American sociologists began to describe the importance of the small primary group of people with whom any given person may interact. [15] Sociologists' reports of such groups are primarily descriptive of uncontrived situations rather than of experimental manipulations of the many variables in group functioning.

---

[10] Harold R. Peat, _Private Peat_ (New York: Harper & Brothers, 1918).

[11] Marion Hargrove, _See Here, Private Hargrove_ (New York: Holt, 1942).

[12] Harold Guetzkow, ed., _Groups, Leadership, and Men_ (Pittsburg: Carnegie Institute Press, 1952).

[13] Elihu Katz and Paul F. Lazarsfeld, _Personal Influence_ (Glencoe, Ill.: Free Press, 1955).

[14] Alvin Gouldner, ed., _Studies in Leadership_ (New York: Harper & Brothers, 1950).

[15] Edward Shils, "The Study of the Primary Group," in _The Policy Sciences_, Daniel Lerner and Harold D. Lasswell, eds. (Stanford: Stanford University Press, 1951), pp. 44-69.

Experimental Evidence of Group Influences on Individuals

Numerous studies clarify the influence of groups on the individual.[16] Some of these studies help to suggest the nature of group influences on perceptions, attitudes, beliefs, aspirations, and behavior.[17]

Perceptions. The effect of the group on its members' perceptions of persons, objects, or situations "out there" in the external world has been established in many laboratory experiments.[18] The classic study is that of Muzafer Sherif.[19] In this study, Sherif used the illusion of movement created by a pinpoint of light that is actually stationary. Each subject in the experiment was taken into a darkened room and asked to estimate the number of inches the light "moved" on each occasion that it was flashed. The apparent movement of the light is called the autokinetic effect.

After each subject had established some kind of personal "norm" estimate of the distance that the light "moved," the subjects were brought together in small groups and the experiment repeated. Although each subject's first few estimates in the group situation were close to the norm he had established when he was alone, he generally modified his estimate until a group norm was established; he then conformed to the group norm although it may have varied from his original estimate. When the experiment was revised, with the group situation preceding the individual estimates, the group norm was accepted by the subjects and taken into the individual situation, where it was modified only slightly. Sherif's experiments are largely responsible for the term frame of reference, which has since gained wide scientific currency. This term indicates that a social norm develops into a standard that is shared by members of the group and against which all things are measured.

Perhaps the most striking evidence of the power of group pressure to alter perception is found in a study of Asch.[20] A group of subjects was shown three lines on a card and asked which of the three lines was similar in length

---

[16]Dorwin Cartwright and Alvin Zander, eds. Group Dynamics (Evanston: Row, Peterson, 1953).

[17]Erland Mindus, Industrial Psychiatry (Geneva: World Health Organization, 1957).

[18]Eugene L. Hartley and Ruth E. Hartley, Fundamentals of Social Psychology (New York: Knopf, 1952), pp. 372-406.

[19]Muzafer Sherif, A Study of Some Social Factors in Perception, Archives of Psychology, 1935, No. 187.

[20]Solomon Asch, Social Psychology (Englewood Cliffs, N.J.: Prentice-Hall, 1952), pp. 450-501.

to a line on another card -- the experimental card. Only one of the three lines was as long as the experimental card's line. Of the nine subjects in the group, all but one were in collusion with the experimenter. They deliberately selected a line that was clearly and very visibly shorter than the experimental card's line by as much as 1-3/4 inches. Thus, the one subject not in collusion with the experimenter found eight other members of the group contradicting the evidence of his own eyes. In these experiments, the erroneous "estimates" of the majority contaminated approximately one-third of the estimates of the subjects; these subjects went along with the clearly erroneous statements of the majority, which were contrary to the evidence of their senses. Since the lines were not more than 15 inches long, the 1-3/4-inch difference was quite substantial. Only one-fourth of the subjects did not modify their perceptions in some way as a result of hearing the observations of the other members of the group. The subjects who yielded to group pressure did so for three different reasons: some actually had their perceptions of the lengths of the lines altered; some could perceive the lines correctly, but their judgment about the lines was distorted; and some knew that the majority was in error but did not wish to appear different from the other group members.

All experiments on group influences show that individuals respond differently to group pressures;[21] as one would expect, there are differences in groups themselves, which are reflected in their differential effects on their members.[22] One experiment showed that groups of high and low cohesiveness respond differently to a common situation.[23] Each group consisted of two individuals. Each group member was instructed to make a report on some photographs and to talk to his partner to see if the partner's report could be improved. The pictures given to each partner had slight differences that permitted different interpretations. Thus, each partner found himself confronting different interpretations from the other. The members of the low cohesive groups generally accepted the differences in interpretation passively. Members of the highly cohesive groups, on the other hand, tried to reconcile their differences when they became aware of them. Interestingly, fewer than half of the subjects in the low cohesive groups but over two-thirds of the subjects in the highly cohesive groups said they had recognized their partners' attempts to influence them. These attempts were more effective in the high than in the low cohesive groups. Thus, the influence of an experience upon an individual

---

[21]Erich Kahler, The Tower and the Abyss (New York: George Braziller, 1957).

[22]Leo Postman and Jerome S. Bruner, "Perception Under Stress," Journal of Personality, 18 (1949), 22-31.

[23]Helen H. Jennings, Leadership and Isolation (New York: Longmans, Green, 1947).

sometimes depends upon the cohesion of the group of which he believes himself a member.[24]

   Attitudes. A person's attitudes mainly reflect the groups to which he belongs. Apparently few people develop attitudes on any subject by thinking it through carefully, considering various solutions to the problem, and selecting their stand solely on the basis of disinterested reasoning. Many people strongly resist this notion, for they are honestly convinced that their thoughts are their very own. It does not require any adherence to "group-think" or to concepts like "other-directedness" to realize the strong effect of group memberships on attitude formation.

   Groups do not influence the attitudes of all their members in the same manner. A person's position in a group is reflected in his response to it.[25] Although most members of a group usually conform to the group's views, some may be nonconformists. In addition, some may conform on most issues but not on others. Such differential conformity may be explained by loyalties to other groups to which people belong. Occasionally, strong pressure -- as from parents or teacher -- to depart from some group position may result in a person's renunciation of the group. Despite this kind of deviation, the most general pattern of response is for people to accept the attitudes of the groups to which they belong and to defend such attitudes in whatever way is most congenial to them.

   A classic study, which clearly shows the impact of the reference group on an individual's attitudes, was made at Bennington College during the 1930s by Theodore Newcomb.[26] In this study, each student's attitudes were measured each year for a four-year period on social issues such as unemployment, public relief, and the rights of organized labor. A large majority of the students came from families whose social attitudes were conservative, but the college atmosphere was decidedly liberal. Accordingly, freshmen as a whole had conservative attitudes on the social issues involved in the study. However, as these freshmen became in turn sophomores, juniors, and seniors, the great majority shifted from their conservative positions to more liberal attitudes. This shift is exemplified by the finding that 62 per cent of the freshmen but only 14 per cent of the upperclasswomen preferred the Republican cause in the 1936 elections, while 29 per cent of the freshmen and 54 per cent of the upperclasswomen preferred the Democrats.

----

[24]Irving L. Janis, Air War and Emotional Stress (New York: McGraw-Hill, 1951).

[25]Alex Bavelas, "Communication Patterns in Task-Oriented Groups," Journal of the Acoustical Society of America, 22 (1950), 725-730.

[26]Theodore M. Newcomb, Personality and Social Change (New York: Dryden, 1943).

As the figures indicate, not all of the Bennington students modified their attitudes toward liberalism as a consequence of group pressure. Some students did not appreciably alter their attitudes, and a few even actively resisted the community's pressure. Those who did shift position did so because they increasingly identified with the college. The campus collectively became their reference group. For those who did not change, however, identification with groups external to the campus remained stronger than that with the college. Friends and family, rather than the college, continued to be their reference group.

Aspirations. Attitudes and perceptions are not the only aspects of behavior that can be changed by group membership. The impact of the group on aspirations has been documented in a number of studies on the socialization of military personnel.[27] One measure often employed is the "level of aspiration," or the individual's expectations of his own performance. In studies of soldiers during World War II, research established that many soldiers entered military service with minimal anticipations of their own role. They planned to do as little work as possible while in the service. After a training period, however, many developed considerable esprit de corps. Their aspirations changed from doing as little as possible to doing as thorough a job as possible. The change in level of aspiration was attributed by the soldiers to the feeling of belonging to a group, and the continuous contact with a highly motivated cadre of training personnel.

Behavior. We have discussed the group's influence on relatively intangible aspects of behavior -- attitudes, perception, and levels of aspiration. Actual behavior is also affected. One effect of the group on the actions of individual members is demonstrated by a study of a department in a plant where one hundred men worked at piece rates.[28] These men received a bonus on all production over 66 per cent of a standard output; but the group had established a rule that no one was to produce over 150 per cent of standard on any job, lest exceeding this output cause a cut in pay rates. A majority of the men consistently earned a bonus, but they never went beyond the 150 per cent output. Only ten men disregarded the rule and produced, on the average, 150-200 per cent of the standard output. This study gives a rough indication of the strength of pressures to conform and the relative infrequency with which individuals deviate from the norms established by a group to which they belong.

In one famous experiment, Kurt Lewin and some colleagues systematically varied the "atmosphere" of various groups, from authoritarian to

[27]Samuel A. Stouffer et al., Combat and Its Aftermath, vol. II of The American Soldier (Princeton: Princeton University Press, 1949).

[28]Orvis Collins, Melville Dalton, and Donald Roy, "Restriction of Output and Social Cleavage in Industry," Applied Anthropology, 5 (1946), 1-14.

democratic to laissez-faire.[29] The experimenters set up small but genuine
children's groups and, over a period of weeks, varied the kind of leadership
that the groups received as they executed their tasks. Clear differences in the
behavior of the groups could be observed; these differences appeared to be
reflections of the kind of leadership that each group received. Authoritarian
groups tended to be either more aggressive or more apathetic than the democratic groups. The authoritarian groups had more submissive approaches to the
leader, as well as more activities that were clearly designed to call attention
to themselves. There were also more aggressive and dominating relations
among the individuals in authoritarian groups. The authoritarian groups had
more "I-feeling," and the democratic groups showed more "We-feeling." The
laissez-faire groups also showed a distinct pattern. The "atmosphere" or
climate of the group thus was visibly translated into behavior on the part of
group members.

Differential effects of group memberships. As has been suggested by
several of the studies cited above, not all members of the same group are
affected in the same way by their membership in the group. Differences in
individual responses to the group can be traced mainly to three factors: the
status of the individual within the group -- that is, whether he is a leader or
a follower; the differences in the tenets and purposes of the other groups to
which the individual belongs; and variations in individual personality traits
and temperament.

The influence of a group upon an individual's behavior, attitudes, and
perceptions varies with the extent to which he feels identified with it.
Leaders are both identified with their group by others and identify themselves
closely with their group; in addition, the need of winning new members to the
group or of eliciting cooperation, effort, or compliance from others in the
group usually has the effect of re-enforcing the leader's own loyalty to the
group.[30] Also, leaders generally derive considerable ego gratification from
their position of leadership and are therefore likely to be very positively dis-
posed toward the group's norms -- much more so than those who are held in
low regard by others in the group.

Individuals belong to many groups that frequently are inconsistent in
some of their norms and pressures. When the conflicts between the norms of
groups to which an individual belongs become great, he generally must choose
between them. Even when there is no conflict among them, membership in
other groups may affect the extent and manner of an individual's conformity to

---

[29]Kurt Lewin, Ronald Lippitt, and Ralph K. White, "Patterns of Aggressive
Behavior in Experimentally Created Social Climates," Journal of Social
Psychology, 10 (1939), 271-299.

[30]John K. Hemphill, Situational Factors in Leadership (Columbus: Ohio State
University, Bureau of Educational Research, 1949).

the pressures of the group. Consequently, individuals belonging to the same group will respond to it differently according to their other group memberships.

Some people are temperamentally rebels or nonconformists for reasons that probably relate to their relationship to their parents, other siblings, and childhood peers. These personal characteristics are likely to be reflected in the way that individuals react to group pressures, and may lead them to adopt attitudes and modes of behavior that run counter to those of a membership group.

APPLICATIONS OF BEHAVIORAL SCIENCE MATERIAL ON GROUPS TO PRICING

The Pricer as a Group Member

The executive responsible for pricing belongs to a large hierarchy of groups. His membership in some of these groups results from the very fact that he is responsible for pricing; he belongs to other groups in his nonprofessional capacity as a father, a member of some church, an athlete, etc. In addition, he belongs to some groups by virtue of the size and character of the firm for which he works. Accordingly, groups to which many pricing executives belong, which are likely to influence his decisions and actions with respect to price, are explored in the following pages. This exploration attempts to assess the effects of group memberships on pricing executives' behavior and the likelihood that group membership causes them to depart from pure economic calculation.

Group memberships within the firm. Informal groupings arise in all large organizations. Because of similarity of interest, recreation, religions, educational background, political affiliations, job responsibilities, propinquity, etc., individuals tend to cluster. These clusters need not be enduring or tightly knit; membership might change frequently. Whatever their basis or duration, such groups exist in all firms and virtually everyone belongs to one or more of them.

The pricing executive belongs to such informal groupings and also to some formal groups. For example, he may be a member of several executive committees, some of which deal with matters related to pricing while others are concerned with other matters. Depending on the number and function of these committees, his knowledge of what is going on in the firm, and of the current plans and anxieties of top management, will vary. Also, his behavior as a member of these committees -- including those concerned with pricing -- will depend upon his status within the firm. If he is regarded by his colleagues as an up-and-coming executive slated for advancement (and shares that view himself), he is likely to behave very differently than if he feels his supervisor is discontented with his performance and that his job is in jeopardy. The up-

and-coming executives might constitute a distinct group within a corporation that inculcated attitudes, shared information, and created general standards. Adherence to the norms of such a group would cause a member of the group to behave quite differently about prices than would an executive who feared he was "on the way out."

Group memberships outside the firm. Business executives generally have links to the industry of which their firm is a part. Relatively few industries are without a trade association and almost all firms subscribe to one or more trade journals; many executives, moreover, hold office in the trade association, or may represent the industry on advisory committees to the government. In these capacities they are likely to strengthen their identification with the industry. Industry conventions, trade shows, and the like, provide meeting places for executives in competing firms and may give rise to special groupings. Also, in some industries that are concentrated geographically, executives of rival firms often are members of the same country club and church. In these many ways, an executive becomes a member of the industry group -- or of several informal industry groups.

Major Group Influences on Pricing Behavior

An executive probably is affected in subtle ways by the industry of which his firm is a part and by the class of firms within the industry to which his firm belongs. By virtue of thinking of himself as a "steel-industry executive" rather than, say, someone in the cloak and suit or meat-packing industry, he identifies with a unique reference group and adopts its behavior norms. His behavior may be affected in various ways as a result. Similarly, if he knows that his firm is regarded as a member of the progressive branch of the industry rather than the conservative segment, he is likely to adapt his behavior accordingly. In a like manner, the personality of the firm itself -- and most firms have one -- is likely to affect an executive's point of view and actions quite as much as its written statement of policies. However, little direct evidence has been collected about those who make price decisions and the extent to which they have been influenced by their memberships in formal and informal groups. It is possible to speculate about these matters, although it should be recognized that speculations in this field are notoriously unreliable.

Intra-firm group influences. In most corporations, the executive responsible for pricing operates as a member of a committee. As a result, he is exposed to the influence of the other members of the committee, even though he may have full and final responsibility for the decision reached -- and indeed may have power to make a decision to which all members of the committee object. On the committee, he will ordinarily find representatives of the firm's manufacturing department, controller's office, and sales division. Typically, the pricing executive has close ties with the sales division and may actually be a member of that division; almost always, he will at one time have discharged some sales duties. In temperament, as well as in his reference grouping, then, the pricer is likely to find his closest ties with executives in the sales department. These executives, typically, are inclined to blame poor sales performance on the fact that they have been required to "charge too much." Their impulse is to favor lower prices. On the other hand, the manufacturing executives often want a cushion to cover contingencies and hesitate to commit themselves to turn out the product at a very low cost -- for frequently they have doubts that they can do so. Similarly, representatives of the controller's office are extremely cost-conscious: they desire that the price be set high enough to cover all costs and contingencies, and they often seem rather unconcerned that sales may be meager at such a price.

In this situation, one may conjecture that the pricer will seek a compromise of the divergent views and, in effect, try to create an awareness in all members of the committee that the pricing function calls for the development of new attitudes. Perhaps his main motive will be to bridge differences of opinion -- so that, in place of the objective of setting the price most advantageous for the firm, he may substitute the goal of finding a price to which all members of the committee might agree. In the process, the pricing executive's personal convictions would be submerged by his desire to create a harmonious committee that "gets its job done quickly with a minimum of disagreement." This desire is likely to be especially great if his superiors -- a group to which he wishes to belong -- seem to place a high value on harmonious personal relations.

It would be incorrect to say that the pricing executive will gain nothing by obtaining committee agreement on a price, even at the sacrifice of his own convictions. The agreement of the group to the decision will give him a feeling of security and a strong defense if his decision is challenged. By going along with the group, he minimizes the risks of "sticking his neck out." The latter course invites finger-pointing by other members of the committee if his decision proves to be incorrect.

On the other hand, the pricing executive -- instead of trying to find a compromise position that will accommodate all members of the committee -- may favor the course advocated by his associates in the sales division. The closer his ties with the members of the sales department, the stronger the pressures to favor their views; also, the greater the risk that they will cease to regard him as one of them if he does not lean in their direction. Contrariwise, the pricing executive may want to establish the fact that his function really demands that he rise above inter-divisional disagreements, and he may seek the respect and acceptance of the group consisting of his "opposite numbers" in other divisions. Such a response to the committee situation would ultimately sever his ties with the sales division.

The foregoing speculations are more than inconclusive; they are actually contradictory. Nevertheless, they lead to one interesting conclusion. When a committee, rather than an individual, is vested with responsibility for pricing, the result would turn out quite differently than if the individual had the responsibility. Also, in the course of accommodating to the wishes of other people, the pricing executive tends to lose sight of his own convictions and preferences.

Inter-firm group influences. The types of formal and informal groups composed of executives from different firms in an industry have already been suggested. We can only conjecture that the pressures of inter-firm group memberships sometimes conflict with membership in a particular firm. If one furthers the interest of his firm, he might injure members of the industry groups to which he belongs. In the absence of informal or formal industry groups, such conflicts would not arise and behavior very possibly would be quite different.

What effects upon price are likely to flow from the existence of such groups? In general terms, the main effect is likely to be a blunting of the competitive urge to injure one's competitors and the creation of a sympathetic understanding and mutual regard for them. It is far easier to steal the customers of anonymous and faceless rivals than to pirate away business from persons with whom one has recently spent a pleasant social evening and will meet again soon.

Economists have noted the widespread existence of price leadership in modern industry. Although they are inclined to attribute this phenomenon to mutual recognition of the benefits of cooperation and the folly of unbridled competition, it can be explained quite as well on grounds of group pressures. Actually, there is no need to choose between these two explanations for price leadership because they probably re-enforce each other; probably neither one would be sufficient in itself to create an enduring price-leadership situation.

It may also be conjectured that the growth of formal and informal groups within industries has contributed to price stability. To alter price would disturb a situation that the other firms apparently regard as satisfactory; unless there were prior consultation -- or a recognized condition of price leadership -- a firm's departure from a prevailing price might easily be interpreted by the other firms as a renunciation of the group. And, as already mentioned, even the firm reducing price could do so only if its executives ceased to regard themselves as "one of the boys." Clearly, "one of the boys" does not depart from a price charged by all other firms: by taking such action, the executives signify that their membership in the industry group has changed, if not ended.

CONCLUSION

VALUE OF PERIPHERAL MATERIALS TO AN UNDERSTANDING OF PRICING

This book has endeavored to enrich our understanding of pricing, to test a method of introducing peripheral materials into business subjects, and to provide one concrete example of what such materials add to understanding. It cannot be overemphasized that no single business subject can possibly be representative of all. Consequently, it would be dangerous to generalize about the value of peripheral materials on the basis of this study. Moreover, no small group -- especially one employing a heretofore unknown approach -- can be considered in any sense typical of other groups that might attempt to incorporate new materials into the field of business. Despite these caveats, as a result of this study we do know considerably more than we could have known otherwise about the value of peripheral materials and the methods of communicating them to students of and specialists in business. What we "know" cannot be considered a firm conclusion by any means; on the other hand, it does represent a hypothesis to be tested -- or used as our "best guess" until challenged by other evidence.

Little need be said about the value of the method employed to search out peripheral materials of possible value to business specialists. The existence of this book proves that it can be made to work. The flaws in this book show that the method is not foolproof. The experience of the team members further attests that the method is not painless. However, the group members (with varying degrees of enthusiasm) endorse the method and pronounce it "almost nice" -- at least, as much fun as washing dishes.

The main purpose of this concluding chapter is to comment on the magnitude and nature of the contributions that operations research and behavioral science make to an understanding of the pricing process. It is hardly surprising that each of these peripheral fields contributes quite different things and in different ways. Consequently, the contributions of each will be discussed separately.

CONTRIBUTIONS OF OPERATIONS RESEARCH
TO AN UNDERSTANDING OF PRICING

The careful reader doubtless has already observed that the chapters dealing with operations research are not parallel to those dealing with behavioral science. Whereas the latter chapters contain sections that explicitly apply the concepts and findings reviewed to pricing, the applicability of the operations research materials to pricing is not discussed. Considerable insight into the occasions when peripheral materials are most valuable can be obtained by understanding why this difference in treatment exists.

There can no longer be any argument against the conclusion that operations research methods have been applied successfully to certain areas of business. However, they have achieved greatest success in areas in which there had previously been little theoretical analysis. In such areas, the quantitative methods developed by operations researchers have ordinarily afforded totally new ways of looking at problems. However, in the area of pricing decisions, there has long existed a large body of carefully reasoned economic analysis; economists have elaborated a very effective way of looking at pricing problems. It is, therefore, extremely unlikely that operations research could supply any generally valid and wholly new concepts that would provide insight into pricing problems; and, as a matter of fact, it does not.

Nonetheless, operations research methods can contribute some insights that will be useful in pricing decisions. In the first place, operations research provides a method of "handling" uncertainty, whereas classical economic theory offers no such method. The economist who deals with pricing problems thus assumes perfect knowledge on the part of the decision-maker. This assumption, of course, is almost never true in practical decision problems and is certainly not true in most pricing problems. On the contrary, the businessman is faced with general uncertainties. Using the economists' terms, we can say that the businessman generally does not know the demand schedule for his product, nor does he know the elasticity of the demand. At best, he may have some knowledge from which he can assign probabilities to various elasticities.

One of the major contributions of operations research, then, is a method of "handling" uncertainty. The whole of decision theory as sketched here can be considered a careful analysis of what constitutes rational behavior in the face of uncertainty. Consequently, familiarity with these approaches will be useful to those who make price decisions as well as to others faced with uncertainty. In this sense, we can say the operations research methods can be superimposed upon and will strengthen a classical economic theory relevant to pricing. They thus afford a basis for extending the theory to cope with the uncertainties of the business reality.

Apart from this, the mere conceptualization of decision problems in terms of a payoff matrix can clarify most decision problems -- even if it is impossible to quantify the payoffs. This statement is the result of experience and cannot be documented. Moreover, as decision problems become complicated by the presence of many controllable factors and many relevant uncontrollable factors, it is very useful to sort them out in the pattern of a payoff matrix. This advantage, of course, is not confined to pricing problems but it is equally true of them.

Finally, it is particularly true of pricing problems that they involve conflict with competitors. This mean, in our terms, that they are similar to games. Although game theory does not contribute a method of forecasting competitors' behavior, we think that such basic ideas of game theory as dominance and mixed strategies are useful aid in thinking about such problems.

The discussion of the competitive bidding model (Chapter 3) does not require any application to pricing; it _is_ pricing. That model demonstrates the possibility of rationally coping with uncertainty about competitors' actions by quantitative methods quite apart from game theory itself.

These, then, are some of the insights regarding pricing problems, which are available from operations research. Although none of them provides a solution to the general pricing problem, it appears, nonetheless, that each of them contributes better understanding of any specific pricing problem. Together, they permit the pricing specialist to take a step in the right direction; and future development in the field of operations research may well result in further steps. Many efforts are currently being made to extend these operations research methods so that pricing problems can be handled better by means of them. In the meantime, we must remain content with some additional insights as aids to our pricing decisions.

CONTRIBUTIONS OF BEHAVIORAL SCIENCE TO AN UNDERSTANDING OF PRICING

As the applications that could be made of behavioral science to pricing were reviewed, no dramatic discoveries were uncovered. The findings of behavioral science were found to be consistent with and to run parallel to experience in the field of business and to conclusions already held by businessmen. It was possible to draw examples from the field of pricing to illustrate most of the generalizations advanced by behavioral science. Thus, behavorial science corroborates and reinforces the conclusions already reached by businessmen; from this one sample, at any rate, it does not suggest new conclusions, nor does it correct views currently held.

The corroborative value of behavioral science findings should not be minimized. Although there is a wealth of business experience upon which students of business conceivably might draw, business secrecy and the tendency of businessmen to be guided by public relations considerations rather than canons of scientific truth often obscure the true nature of what happens in business and the conclusions reached by business executives. Consequently, there probably are some areas in which behavioral science findings suggest what happens in business and inform outsiders about what is already known to many business practitioners.

-120-

Probably the greatest contribution of behavioral science to pricing (and to business in general) consists in sharpening and strengthening the conclusions held by business specialists. Many of the findings of behavioral science are based upon carefully designed surveys with, if anything, excessive preoccupation with methodology. In contrast, businessmen, and even most close students of business, have not attempted to derive generalizations from business experience by careful experimentation and scientific observation. Consequently, by blending what is known about business with the methods and findings of behavioral science, business specialists probably can obtain a clearer and more powerful body of concepts and empirical generalizations. Familiarity with the methods of the behavioral scientist, moreover, cannot help but make the student of business much more conscious of his methods of analysis and more critical of the broad generalizations to which he is so often exposed about business. The result might well be to create a far more scientific approach to business, which probably will yield great benefits to the behavioral scientist; for the world of business offers enormous and largely unexploited opportunities to learn about human behavior.

A critical question that must be faced by university administrators, college professors, and business consultants is how much value to attach to the kinds of behavioral science contributions and applications to business that have been pointed out here. It is not enough to argue that their value is greater than zero. One must measure their value against the substantial costs involved in absorbing them. More specifically, one must decide whether, from the standpoint of students or clients, greater resources must be devoted to behavioral science or to such things as operations research, economic theory, market research techniques -- or possibly other areas.

This kind of comparison is extremely difficult, and the answer may vary for each school, business, and consulting firm. The appropriate decision for each will depend on its particular needs; it is unlikely to be the same for the total field of business. That is, a teacher of pricing is likely to include far less behavioral science, for example, than a teacher of consumer behavior. Similarly, executives working with organizational problems presumably will find much greater use for behavioral science than will executives specializing in corporate finance.

In addition to placing a value on the application of behavioral science to schools of business and in executive training programs, it is necessary to find an efficient method of doing so. It seems exceedingly unlikely that one can best meet this problem by simply teaching behavioral science and expecting students or practitioners to make applications to their specialties. Rather, to make this decision about method, one must balance many factors -- not the least of which are the skills of the faculty, the training that students and executives bring with them, and the particular subject matter involved.

INDEX